JEFFERSON'S CALL FOR NATIONHOOD

Library of Presidential Rhetoric

Martin J. Medhurst, General Editor

———◆•◆•◆———

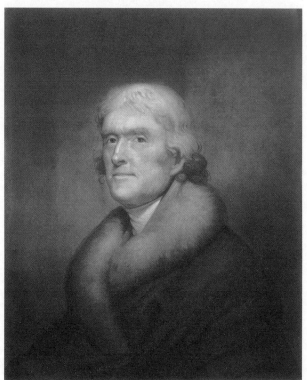

Reproduced from the original painting by Rembrandt Peale through the courtesy of the New York Historical Society

Jefferson's
Call for Nationhood

The First Inaugural Address

STEPHEN HOWARD BROWNE

Texas A&M University Press : College Station

Cover Illustration and Frontispiece: Library of Congress,
Prints and Photographs Division, Presidential File. Reproduction Number:
LC-USZC4-2474. This print is a reproduction of the 1805
Rembrandt Peale painting of Thomas Jefferson held by
the New York Historical Society.

Library of Congress Cataloging-in-Publication Data

Brown, Stephen H.
    Jefferson's call for nationhood : the first inaugural address /
Stephen Howard Browne.—1st ed.
        p. cm.—(Library of presidential rhetoric)
    Includes bibliographical references and index.
    ISBN 1-58544-251-8 (alk. paper)—
    ISBN 1-58544-252-6 (pbk. : alk. paper)
        1. United States—Politics and government—1801–1809.
    2. Jefferson, Thomas, 1743–1826—Political and social views.
    3. Jefferson, Thomas, 1743–1826—Language.   4. Jefferson,
    Thomas, 1743–1826—Oratory.   5. Presidents—United States—
    Inaugural addresses.   6. Rhetoric—Political aspects—United
    States—History—18th century.   7. Discourse analysis—
    United States.   I. Title.   II. Series.
    E332.77.B76   2003
    352.23'86'097309034—dc21   2002152894

In Memoriam

———◆•●•◆———

Mary Ellen Browne

(1920–2001)

David Edwin Browne

(1919–2001)

Contents

Acknowledgments

So slender a volume ought not to suggest paucity of support. Indeed, it could not have been written without the contributions, some silent, of the many scholars with whom it has been my great fortune to work through the years. Marty Medhurst first encouraged me to undertake this study, and he has remained a friend of the project and its author throughout. Robert Ferguson and James Farrell provided expert commentary on the draft; while I may not have risen to their call at every point, I am very grateful for their insights and suggestions. A long time ago, Stephen Lucas introduced me not only to the early republic, but to standards of scholarship suited to its study. He may not approve of the result as embodied here, but his work has served this book as a model of historical and critical inquiry. As always, I am grateful for the psychic support—and challenges—from those most important to me: Margaret, Jessica, Maria, Emily, and Elizabeth, republicans too.

Thomas Jefferson's
First Inaugural Address
March 4, 1801

Friends and fellow-citizens,

Called upon to undertake the duties of the first executive office of our country, I avail myself of the presence of that portion of my fellow-citizens which is here assembled to express my grateful thanks for the favor with which they have been pleased to look toward me, to declare a sincere consciousness that the task is above my talents, and that I approach it with those anxious and awful presentiments which the greatness of the charge and the weakness of my powers so justly inspire. A rising nation, spread over a wide and fruitful land, traversing all the seas with the rich productions of their industry, engaged in commerce with nations who feel power and forget right, advancing rapidly to destinies beyond the reach of mortal eye—when I contemplate these transcendent objects, and see the honor, the happiness, and the hopes of this beloved country committed to the issue and the auspices of this day, I shrink from the contemplation, and humble myself before the magnitude of the undertaking. Utterly, indeed, should I despair did not the presence of many whom I here see remind me that in the other high authorities provided by our Constitution I shall find resources of wisdom, of virtue, and of zeal on which to rely under all difficulties. To you, then, gentlemen, who are charged with the sovereign functions of legislation, and to those associated with you, I look with encouragement for that guidance and support which may enable us to steer with safety the vessel in which we are all embarked amidst the conflicting elements of a troubled world.

During the contest of opinion through which we have passed the animation of discussions and of exertions has sometimes worn an aspect which might impose on strangers unused to think freely and to speak and to write what they think; but this being now decided by the voice of the nation, announced according to the rules of the Constitution, all will, of course, arrange themselves under the will of the law, and unite in common efforts for the common good. All, too, will bear in mind this sacred principle, that though the will of the majority is in all cases to prevail, that will to be rightful must be reasonable; that the minority possess their equal rights, which equal law must protect, and to violate would be oppression. Let us, then, fellow-citizens, unite with one heart and one mind. Let us restore to social intercourse that harmony and affection without which liberty and even life itself are but dreary things. And let us reflect that, having banished from our land that religious intolerance under which mankind so long bled and suffered, we have yet gained little if we countenance a political intolerance as despotic, as wicked, and capable of as bitter and bloody prosecutions. During the throes and convulsions of the ancient world, during the agonizing spasms of infuriated man, seeking through blood and slaughter his long-lost liberty, it was not wonderful that the agitation of the billows should reach even this distant and peaceful shore; that this should be more felt and feared by some and less by others, and should divide opinions as to measures of safety. But every difference of opinion is not a difference of principle. We have called by different names brethren of the same principle. We are all Republicans, we are all Federalists. If there be any among us who would wish to dissolve this Union or to change its republican form, let them stand undisturbed as monuments of the safety with which error of opinion may be tolerated where reason is left free to combat it. I know, indeed, that some honest men fear that a republican government can not be strong, that this Government is not strong enough; but would the honest patriot, in the full tide of successful experiment, abandon a government which has so far kept us free and firm on the theoretic and visionary fear that this Government, the world's best hope, may by possibility want energy to preserve itself? I trust not. I believe this, on the contrary, the strongest Government on earth. I believe it is the only one where every man, at the call of the law, would fly to the standard of the law, and would meet invasions of the public order as his own personal concern. Sometimes it is said that man can not be trusted with the government of himself. Can he, then, be trusted with the government of others? Or have we found angels in the forms of kings to govern him? Let history answer this question.

Let us, then, with courage and confidence pursue our own Federal and Republican principles, our attachment to union and representative government. Kindly separated by nature and a wide ocean from the exterminating havoc of one quarter of the globe; too high-minded to endure the degradations of the others; possessing a chosen country, with room enough for our descendants to the thousandth and thousandth generation; entertaining a due sense of our equal right to the use of our faculties, to the acquisitions of our own industry, to honor and confidence from our fellow-citizens, resulting not from birth, but from our actions and their sense of them; enlightened by a benign religion, professed, indeed, and practiced in various forms, yet all of them inculcating honesty, truth, temperance, gratitude, and the love of man; acknowledging and adoring an overruling Providence, which by all its dispensations proves that it delights in the happiness of man here and his greater happiness hereafter—with all these blessings, what more is necessary to make us a happy and a prosperous people? Still one thing more, fellow-citizens—a wise and frugal Government, which shall restrain men from injuring one another, shall leave them otherwise free to regulate their own pursuits of industry and improvement, and shall not take from the mouth of labor the bread it has earned. This is the sum of good government, and this is necessary to close the circle of our felicities.

About to enter, fellow-citizens, on the exercise of duties which comprehend everything dear and valuable to you, it is proper you should understand what I deem the essential principles of our Government, and consequently those which ought to shape its Administration. I will compress them within the narrowest compass they will bear, stating the general principle, but not all its limitations. Equal and exact justice to all men, of whatever state or persuasion, religious or political; peace, commerce, and honest friendship with all nations, entangling alliances with none; the support of the State governments in all their rights, as the most competent administrations of our domestic concerns and the surest bulwarks against antirepublican tendencies; the preservation of the General Government in its whole constitutional vigor, as the sheet anchor of our peace at home and safety abroad; a jealous care of the right of election by the people—a mild and safe corrective of abuses which are lopped by the sword of revolution where peaceful remedies are unprovided; absolute acquiescence in the decisions of the majority, the vital principle of republics, from which is no appeal but to force, the vital principle and immediate parent of despotism; a well-disciplined militia, our best reliance in peace and for the first moments of war till regulars may relieve them; the supremacy of the civil over the military authority; economy in the public expense, that labor may be lightly burthened; the honest payment of our debts and sacred preservation of the public faith; encouragement of agriculture, and of commerce as its handmaid; the diffusion of information and arraignment of all abuses at the bar of the public reason; freedom of religion; freedom of the press, and freedom of person under the protection of the habeas corpus, and trial by juries impartially selected. These principles form the bright constellation which has gone before us and guided our steps through an age of revolution and reformation. The wisdom of our sages and blood of our heroes have been devoted to their attainment. They should be the creed of our political faith, the text of civic instruction, the touchstone by which to try the services of those we trust; and should we wander from them in moments of error or of alarm, let us hasten to retrace our steps and to regain the road which alone leads to peace, liberty, and safety.

I repair, then, fellow-citizens, to the post you have assigned me. With experience enough in subordinate offices to have seen the difficulties of this the greatest of all, I have learnt to expect that it will rarely fall to the lot of imperfect man to retire from this station with the reputation and the favor which bring him into it. Without pretensions to that high confidence you reposed in our first and greatest revolutionary character, whose preeminent services had entitled him to the first place in his country's love and destined for him the fairest page in the volume of faithful history, I ask so much confidence only as may give firmness and effect to the legal administration of your affairs. I shall often go wrong through defect of judgment. When right, I shall often be thought wrong by those whose positions will not command a view of the whole ground. I ask your indulgence for my own errors, which will never be intentional, and your support against the errors of others, who may condemn what they would not if seen in all its parts. The approbation implied by your suffrage is a great consolation to me for the past, and my future solicitude will be to retain the good opinion of those who have bestowed it in advance, to conciliate that of others by doing them all the good in my power, and to be instrumental to the happiness and freedom of all.

Relying, then, on the patronage of your good will, I advance with obedience to the work, ready to retire from it whenever you become sensible how much better choice it is in your power to make. And may that Infinite Power which rules the destinies of the universe lead our councils to what is best, and give them a favorable issue for your peace and prosperity.

JEFFERSON'S CALL FOR NATIONHOOD

Introduction

Late in the morning of March 4, 1801, the tall, fair, and conspicuously informal Virginian walked several hundred yards from his lodgings to mount the steps of the unfinished Capitol. Accompanied by a small but impressive parade of militia officers, Thomas Jefferson made his way to the Senate chamber dressed, as Henry Adams recounted, as "a plain citizen, without any distinctive badge of office." The president-elect was received by approximately a thousand supporters, congressmen, and the curious, most of whom had no chance of actually hearing the soft-spoken leader of the Republican Party. Greeting him, too, were Aaron Burr, who had been sworn in as vice president earlier that morning, and John Marshall, the dour Chief Justice whose task this day was to administer to his Republican relative the oath of office. It was a trio gathered out of obligation alone, and now, as Adams put it, "the assembled senators looked up at three men who profoundly disliked and distrusted each other."[1]

The words Jefferson spoke that day may have done little to dispel personal resentments, but when he finished the nation knew itself to have witnessed a masterpiece. At 1716 words, forty-one sentences, and seven paragraphs the address did not take long to deliver; indeed no student of Jefferson's rhetorical art would have expected otherwise. In its "language, its perspicuity, its arrangement, its felicity of thought and expression," wrote one observer, the inaugural address was "a model of eloquence," a virtuoso performance by "one of the best writers which our country has produced." The principles Jefferson enshrined that day, reported the *Independent Chronicle,* were "compressed within such precise limits, as to enforce them on the memory, and expressed with such classical elegance, as to charm the scholar with their rhetorical brilliancy." News of the address soon traveled to distant ports, where French supporters in particular welcomed its universal message of conciliation, peace, and republican virtue. "Your message," Pierre Samuel DuPont Nemour declared to Jefferson, "like all your thoughts and writings, is full of wisdom, judgment, and illumination, and contains a divine moral." Jefferson himself, characteristically modest, hoped that the address "will present the leading objects to be conciliation and adherence to sound principle." History records the speaker to have succeeded.[2]

Widely celebrated in its own time, the first inaugural address continues to command the regard of Americans from across the political spectrum. And for much the same reason: it took as its task the subordination of local and temporary interests to the general and abiding principles of republican government. In 1837, George Tucker observed the distinctive manner in which Jefferson's boldness was tempered by that quality of refined understatement we have come to attach to most of his writings. "Though couched in language of humility, and breathing the spirit of benevolence and liberality," Tucker wrote, the address nevertheless "asserts all the cardinal principles of the republican faith, but in such general terms as not to alarm the fears or irritate the prejudices of his opponents." More than half a century after its delivery, Henry Randall found the circulation of its maxims in the press and popular letters to be "astonishing, and perhaps unequaled in the instance of any similar production."[3]

By the twentieth century, far removed from the bitter party struggles and uncertainties from which it emerged and to which it immediately spoke, the address was fully enshrined into the canonical literature of American nationhood. To the populist Tom Watson, Jefferson's speech "will always be to good government what the Sermon on the Mount is to religion," and Woodrow Wilson noted, "Nothing could exceed the fine tact and gentleness with which Mr. Jefferson gave tone of order and patriotic purpose in his inaugural address to the new way of government his followers expected of him." Fawn Brodie judged the address to be "one of the great seminal papers in American political history," indeed of "almost Biblical impact." Jefferson's masterpiece stands today, in the word of the distinguished Jefferson scholar Peter Onuf, as "one of the great texts in the American libertarian tradition, a blast against 'political intolerance and persecution.'"[4]

The significance, stature, and abiding appeal of Jefferson's inaugural address is now universally acknowledged; how curious, then, that it has yet to receive sustained and systematic analysis. This book represents an attempt to initiate that process. I offer it as an introduction to those who are interested in Jefferson and the address in particular but who may not have found occasion to dwell on its origins, composition, meaning, and delivery. Drawing both from primary historical sources and the rich scholarship on Jefferson, I set in place relevant contextual information and submit the text to a series of detailed interpretations. The result, I hope, is to make available a resource for those wishing to enrich their understanding of the address, feature it for classroom discussion, and further their pursuits into the Jeffersonian legacy.

What follows will soon enough announce its own limitations. If nothing else, an entire book—even so slender a volume as this—on such a brief speech will inevitably draw unfavorable comparisons between the felicity of its subject and that of the author. That is fair. My only excuse rests in the conviction that Jefferson's text will reward the effort, that it is so artistically wrought, so culturally resonant and compelling as to justify the attempt. There is, as well, the matter of situating what he says and what gets said about him in the corpus of Jeffersonian scholarship. That scholarship is, to put it mildly, extensive and endlessly suggestive of what might else be said of this or that issue. I have tried to invoke as much of this scholarship as is possible given my aims, argument, and constraints. Needless to say, that much is still but a tiny fraction of the whole. For those curious to explore Jefferson, his world, and his inaugural address at greater length, I have included a fairly extensive bibliography. Here, too, it should be acknowledged that it is necessarily selective; indeed, work now under way and soon to be published will inevitably add to or challenge some of the views contained here.

And then there is the vexed issue of Jefferson's status in the pantheon of American founders, especially as it involves questions surrounding his relationship to slavery. Recent revelations and disputes regarding Jefferson and Sally Hemings, dramatic as they are for many, represent only one aspect of a more general reassessment of the man and his legacy. Academic conferences, publically aired debates, books, exhibitions, and other forums of exchange continue to place Jefferson at the center of controversy. As Merrill Peterson made clear in *The Jefferson Image in the American Mind,* this preoccupation with the meaning, so to speak, of the third president is scarcely new; in fact it dates to his own life time and has seldom if ever abated. In treating at such length one of Jefferson's most important statements on the grounds and prospects of American liberty, I wish not to skirt the question as to how Jefferson could say the things he said even as he held several hundred human beings in bondage. In the old days, one might expect at this point the usual qualifiers: yes, but he treated them well; yes, but he once conceived a plan to eliminate the system; yes, but he was a man of his time and place; yes, but . . . . Such protests no longer convince, if they ever did, and students of Jefferson tend now to confront the issue more openly. Dogged defense can still be heard, of course, as can sweeping condemnation. The more productive alternative, in my view, faces the fact of Jefferson's complicity in the benighted system, acknowledges the force and extent of his vision for an "empire of liberty," and sees the man as embodying some of the best and worst qualities of the American experience. At the same time, I have not for the purposes of this study centered the issue of slavery in my interpretation of the inaugural; to do so, it seemed to me, would be to simply repeat interminably that it was not conceived as applying to large numbers of inhabitants of the republic, among them African Americans of either gender, women of any "race," and Native Americans whatsoever. That is a very important thing to say and remember, but my hope is to say much more and many different things about this remarkable speech.[5]

That said, the following account is undertaken from a perspective broadly construed as rhetorical. By this I refer to a persistent interest in the ways language works to shape our understanding of the world and our relationship to it. To make sense of human action from this view is to emphasize the centrality of symbols in setting the horizons and limits of life, especially as it is lived among others in the conduct of public affairs. Recent scholarship on the role of rhetoric in eighteenth- and nineteenth-century America reflects a similar set of interests: Jay Fliegelman's *Declaring Independence,* Sandra Gustafson's *Eloquence is Power,* Thomas Gustafson's *Representative Words,* Michael Warner's *The Letters of the Republic,* and other works have taught us much about the play of language in shaping the cultural life of the period. My study shares that concern generally and is indebted to this scholarship; at the same time, it differs by attending carefully and at considerable length to the interpretation of a single text. In this book, rhetoric refers to the artistic management of symbols and the cultural traditions from which they draw authority. If there is a lurking theoretical stance organizing the analysis, it is perhaps best captured in Aristotle's conception of rhetoric as "the ability, in each [particular] case, to see the available means of persuasion." There are many other useful definitions of the art, to be sure, but Aristotle's seems to grasp what I take to be central to our understanding of Jefferson and his speech. Above all, it draws attention to a particular kind of intelligence, a capacity to reason and speak effectively in the shifting contexts of political life. This faculty will be exercised best, Aristotle teaches us, when it is trained on the "available means of persuasion," the common store of knowledge and beliefs that in turn become instruments of persuasion.[6]

There are other ways of getting at Jefferson's particular genius, but this stress on rhetoric as the art of effective expression gives us the means to explain a great deal. In particular, it leads us to ask after the interplay of arguments, appeals, and imagery that make up the address; stresses its pragmatic and instrumental character; and invites us to attend to the complex field of operations within which the text embeds itself. As with any trained perspective, this focus on the rhetorical dimensions of Jefferson's address will perforce leave out much; on the other hand, it gives us an opportunity to examine at close range the distinctive achievement of the speech as an act of public persuasion.

The guiding assumption behind the analysis and design of this book is that the first inaugural address is best read not through one but several lenses. Each orientation allows us to rotate our object, prismlike, in order to see its multiple facets, to set it within different contexts and ask different questions as to its sources, meaning, and implications. Our general approach, again, is rhetorical; that is, we will examine the text with a sharp eye for the strategic deployment of arguments, appeals, and imagery. This mode of interpretation allows us to assemble under its auspices diverse but interdependent orientations. These orientations respectively situate the text as (1) a partisan act, the chief function of which is to announce in the most compelling terms possible the victory of the Republicans over and against their Federalist opponents; (2) a statement of political theory, the chief function of which is to reestablish the first principles of republican government; and (3) a rhetorical performance, the chief function of which is to give to both these partisan and theoretical aims their optimal expression. A brief summary of each will help set our coordinates for the chapters that follow. The chapter analyses take as their point of departure certain problems for the student of Jefferson; rather than sweep these under the rug, I have chosen to feature them as interesting in their own right and essential to our understanding of the first inaugural address.

With respect to the partisan ambitions at work in the address, we are confronted immediately with Jefferson's long-held convictions about the dangers of party. Like virtually everyone in the eighteenth century, Jefferson loathed the very idea of party, and he spent the decade preceding his election lambasting those who he claimed were subverting legitimate government through partisan maneuvering. "If I could not go to heaven but with a party," he once declared, "I would not go there at all." The record is not clear on how things finally turned out for the deistic Jefferson on this score, but it is very clear that he in fact was largely responsible for the development and success of America's first great opposition party. The inaugural address itself can plausibly be read as a veritable manifesto of the Republican creed, the single most powerful and eloquent statement ever rendered on behalf of an organized political agenda. Was Jefferson, as his many critics charged, a hypocrite? Deluded? Did he manage somehow to transcend the very political realities that elevated him to the executive office? I leave that to the reader to decide, but offer in chapter one a basis on which to think through the question.[7]

When it comes to discussing Jefferson's text as a political treatise we find ourselves on no less tenuous grounds. The problem is not that we are dealing with a speech rather than a philosophical tome: we have only to think of Edmund Burke to recognize that the two genres are not necessarily incommensurable. No, the problem rests in thinking of Jefferson as a "philosophical" thinker (as we would now say—in his time philosophy referred to natural science) in the first place: he claimed no such status, was seldom original and often slippery when it came to systematic reflection on ideas and theoretical precepts. If there is theory at work in Jefferson's pronouncements it was of the axiomatic kind. His was the faculty, as Charles Francis Adams wrote, "of leading the many, by impressing their minds with happily concentrated propositions." At the same time, we cannot miss in his thought a structure of ideas and ideals that ordered his public statements in ways not arbitrary, not just the clutching of truisms in the face of political need. The first inaugural address rather is notable precisely for its elegant distillation of something very like a public philosophy, the terms and appeal of which no one was better suited to express than the Sage of Monticello. In chapter two, I suggest that, squinted at in the right light, Jefferson's text can be usefully read as the production of a serious and accomplished thinker. He may have been no Montesquieu, no Rousseau, not even an Adams; but he was, unlike these more reflective figures, a theorist of formidable popular appeal.[8]

There is, finally, the matter of Jefferson's place in the rhetorical culture of late-eighteenth and early-nineteenth-century America. Again, the case against locating him there in any prominent way is not too difficult to launch. Jefferson was, by his own reckoning and by consensus, no orator. That station was the rightful claim of Patrick Henry, Richard Henry Lee, and Sam Adams. Jefferson, by marked contrast, was reticent to a fault, abhorred debate and verbal contest, and possessed a skin as thin as any president before or since. But perhaps we need another way of looking at the question, assistance for which we can turn to Jefferson's friend and rival John Adams. "Eloquence in public assemblies is not the surest road to fame and preferment," Adams noted, "unless it be used with caution, very rarely, and with great reserve." Adams, for whom caution and reserve were fleeting indeed, reasoned that "the examples of Washington, Franklin, and Jefferson, are enough to show that silence and reserve in public, are more efficacious than argumentation and oratory." That may be overstating the case a bit, but it does suggest that we need to rethink our terms when explaining the rhetorical culture of Jefferson's day. If, as I argue in chapter three, his inaugural address reached the heights of eloquence, then we are required to identify expectations and apply standards appropriate not to a Patrick Henry but to Jefferson and the ideals for which he stood.[9]

The partisan, the theoretical, and the oratorical are, it is important to stress, intractably related, and I have no wish to pose differences where none belong. To the contrary, I hope to show that by looking at Jefferson's inaugural address in these ways, we can discern a good deal of its multiform textures, its alternating energies and protean shapes. Together, the partisan, philosophical, and rhetorical dimensions of the speech work together to create what is rightfully judged among the greatest achievements of our republican legacy.

A few words, finally, about the labor required in reading the pages ahead. Jefferson's address, as previously noted, has yet to be analyzed with the detail it invites. Historians have provided us with a wealth of contextual information, and have said many useful things about the speech. I have drawn heavily and gratefully from their work. But as to the painstaking process of interpreting the text line by line—sometimes word by word—that is the business of this book, and it will require no small amount of patience. The challenge is compounded by the brevity of the text, and in submitting it to three levels of interpretation, the dangers of redundancy seem at times inescapable. For this I must apologize in advance to the reader and ask for more than the usual indulgence accorded textual critics. By way of mitigating some of the problem, I seek to locate the speech in its relevant political, theoretical, and rhetorical contexts; typically, I have tried to balance each chapter by devoting about half its pages to such contextual determinants and the other half to the speech itself. This too runs a certain danger: why, it may be asked, must we wade through so much extraneous material to get to the real goods? At this point I can only assure the reader that such considerations are not in fact extraneous but key to a fuller grasp of the object. Rhetorical texts, especially one so crafted as Jefferson's, reward sustained attention to their internal dynamics; at the same time, they take on their full meaning and force because they are responses to and projections of prevailing historical and situational factors. Ideally, we seek to have it both ways: to appreciate the singularity of Jefferson's production and its function within broader cultural contexts.

CHAPTER 1

"Brethren of the Same Principle"

The First Inaugural Address

and the Language of Party

John Quincy Adams was not, by any measure, an impressionable man. But after seven years abroad, he could not upon his return to American shores but feel pleasantly surprised at the prospect before him. "The appearance of our country," he wrote Rufus King in October of 1801, "has very much improved since I left it in 1794. I find everywhere the marks of peace within our walls, and prosperity within our palaces— for palaces they may truly be called, those splendid and costly mansions which since my departure seem to have shot up from the earth by enhancement." Indeed there was much to be impressed about. No war, no "entangling alliances," domestic tranquility, a new administration constitutionally secured: small wonder that Adams could take at least momentary satisfaction in the appearance of his country. The nation was poised to grow in population, territorial expanse, commerce, and international prestige in ways only dreamed by previous generations. All America, it seemed, might join in a collective celebration of this, her second revolution: "O'er vast Columbia's varied clime / Her cities, forests, shores, and dales / In shining majesty sublime / Immortal Liberty prevails."[1]

But appearances could be deceiving, and all the sanguinity of spirit expressed by Adams and others could not hide the fact that the nation had been through a period of unprecedented turmoil. The patriotic glow that had surrounded her birth had very quickly given way to an early childhood more tumultuous, more vulnerable, and uncertain than any but the most disaffected might have anticipated. Virtually every year of the republic's first decade had witnessed crises that threatened to stall, reverse, or at least retard the new nation's ascent into maturity. Vociferous attacks on Alexander Hamilton's economic designs, financial panic, local uprisings and the appearance of suspicious democratic societies, fears of undue French and British influence, factional strife, foreign intrigue, legislation oppressive to civil rights, threats of secession—scarcely what the Founding Fathers had in mind in those more auspicious days when the "Spirit of '76" was known to reign. In the starkest of contrasts to Adams's America of 1801, the 1790s were marked by a relentless struggle between highly articulate, deeply antagonistic spokesmen for two different and incompatible visions for what America was to become. The results could be mortifying. "Throughout American political life," John Howe observes, "in the public press, in speeches, sermons, the private correspondence of individuals—there ran a spirit of intolerance and fearfulness that seems quite amazing." It was a life that quickly became "gross and distorted, characterized by heated exaggeration and haunted by conspiratorial fantasy. Events were viewed in apocalyptic terms with the very survival of republican liberty riding in the balance." By 1797, matters had come to the point where political difference had devolved into a particularly venomous civil discord. "Men who have been intimate all their lives," lamented Thomas Jefferson, "cross the street to avoid meeting, and turn their heads another way, lest they should be obliged to touch their hats."[2]

Thomas Jefferson's inaugural address cannot, in this context, be fully understood except as a rhetorical performance of the most complex and portentous kind. Elegant, brief, evincing all the felicities characteristic of Jefferson's prose, the address was known then as it is now to be the singular expression of a nation's highest ideals. Friends and a notable number of foes recognized that they had been made witness

to something very important, something without precedent or analogue in the republic's short history. Above all they heard in the address's
eloquent refrains a call to a better version of themselves as fellow citizens; they had been retrieved, as it were, from a debased and artificially
contentious habit of public life. From every quarter of the nation readers learned that the new president had summoned Americans to a level
above partisanship, beyond acrimony, to a place they had quite nearly
forgotten existed. The typically skeptical *New England Palladium* conceded that "when the speech appeared, we received it as the profession
of a man, who knew that he had been suspected and dreaded, as an
enemy to the government, and who, from motives of interest and policy,
felt the necessity of securing the favorable opinion of his political ad-
versaries. "This," the paper concluded, "was wise and prudent."[3]

While Jefferson's traditional enemies tentatively acknowledged the
restraint of his inaugural address, his supporters were unbounded in
their praise. Again, we can read in that praise a collective sense of
gratitude that, through Jefferson's words, peace of a kind had been
secured, that the exhausting hostilities of the past decade had been
superseded by a higher ambition that was America's own. In Philadelphia, citizens read that the views expressed were "honorable to the
man, and afford the most favorable prognostics to the friends of their
country. Should they be realized," the *Gazette of the United States*
noted, "we shall yet be prosperous and happy. The factious, imperious, the clamorous and the turbulent will still be held in check and
compelled to submit to law instead of exercising lawless domination."
More positively, the address was seen to articulate—or rather to re-
articulate—those principles that had originally inspired Americans
to assume their station among the powers of the earth, to embrace
what God and nature had given to them, ultimately, to make themselves worthy of such a gift. "The Address of President Jefferson," wrote
the *Salem Impartial Register,* "will remain with posterity. His prospect of our rising country inspires our ambition, his views of conflicting opinion, recalls to mind the ocean obedient to its laws even
in the tempest. The happy world of men lies before him, while he
defines the true principles of civil government, and when he com-

mands our confidence in them, he makes us perceive that this happy world is our own."[4]

Such testimonies may be multiplied several times over, but they are perhaps enough to underscore the nearly universal impression that the lasting achievement of Jefferson's address was its elevation. As it rose, so did his listeners and readers, and so do we rise still. Now, that is in a way a simple observation, a summary view of a very complex rhetorical performance, and it will require for its explication in the pages ahead a good deal of elaboration. At this point, it may prove useful to pose, if not an argumentative thesis exactly, at least a point of view and a more or less plausible approach to the analysis of Jefferson's text. Our first order of business in this regard is pressured by what I have represented as the elevated quality of Jefferson's speech, its demonstration that, though born of political strife, it ultimately superintends the conditions of its own making. That much is unmistakable, but we shall lose sight of the complexity of the text should we leave it at that. Jefferson's speech, by consensus something a good deal more than a mere speech, is yet a speech: it is a profoundly political act, in motive, function, and form. For all its readily observable features as a ritualized affirmation of unity, its ceremonial trappings and conciliatory tone, for all, that is, of the seemingly apolitical pretensions we have come to associate with inaugural addresses—for all of this, here is a speech that undertakes to extraordinary effect political work *even as it elides that work.*

When Jefferson rose before his audience to deliver his address, he spoke "in tones so quiet, so sweet and sincere of accent," Woodrow Wilson wrote admiringly, "as to calm every mind they touched." At the heart of this effort to still the passions of the people was a single sentence, the most memorable of the address, and the key to unlocking its partisan genius: "We are all republicans, we are all federalists." Those eight words, it is not too much to say, captured as no other in this exquisitely crafted address the essence of Jefferson's vision for American polity: a nation unified in common conviction, pursuing the same ends, animated not by party ambition but by principles definitively republican, definitively American. Certainly to his supporters, the sentiment offered belated respite from the contagion of partisanship, a disease, seemingly, of European origins but which had taken up host in the republican body politic for going on a decade. "At a time when party spirit had gone abroad," wrote "Ephraim" for the *Gazette of the United States,* "pervaded and inflamed the whole political body, and excited such exacerbation of civil mania as threatened a fatal termination, we see a physician step forward, allay the febrile paroxysm, and proceed to effect a cure by assuaging remedies." The speech was announced to the citizens of Salem as striking "factions dumb," while Philadelphians read that "a cessation of party animosity was for a time complete, and from the tears which bedewed many manly cheeks, and the union of opinion in applause, there appeared to be a total, and a prospect of perpetual annihilation of party passions."[5]

But of course no "revolution," even one so efficient as that which Jefferson later hailed as ushering in his administration, is secured without dissent. Some opponents, like Theodore Dwight, later gave Jefferson no quarter whatever to the new president, who, "like all other demagogues, made use of unworthy, indirect, and servile means to gain popular favor, with the view of accomplishing his ambitious projects." Alexander Hamilton, having lost as much as anyone in the tide of Republican victory, proved willing at least to let Jefferson's words stand as a reproach to any further designs against party intrigue. He thus professed to view the speech "as virtually a candid retraction of past misapprehensions, and a pledge to the community that the new President will not lend himself to dangerous innovations, but in essential points will tread in the steps of his predecessors." Others testified to the inaugural's "lullaby effect" and the danger it posed to an unsuspecting populace. Noah Webster accordingly wrote to Jefferson that "the great body of people, who are of pure minds and easy credulity, found in your address much reason to console themselves on the change of administration. They beheld with pleasure," Webster cautiously noted, "a spirit of conciliation and a cheerful acquiescence, on the part of your opposers, whose tendency was to heal the wounds which party spirit had inflicted on the public tranquility." For all the nicely turned phrases and elevated sentiments, for all the talk of being both Federalists and Republicans, the inaugural was for Jefferson's many enemies the very embodiment of partisan duplicity. If the new president had any doubts as to the residual animosities he was to face in the years ahead, the *Gazette of the United States* was there to inform him—and Americans everywhere—otherwise:

> President Jefferson has made an inaugural speech, and those who ask for comforting words and general professions that mean nothing, because they mean everything, have enjoyed some delightful dreams in consequence of those assurances, that we are all Federalists all Republicans; harmony is to be cultivated, and the spirit of Jacobinism is to be conjured down, and rest satisfied, while hunger gnaws without the bread of office.... But political professions are as empty, as counterfeit as ever.[6]

As with Jefferson's contemporaries, historians have subjected his famous words to varying and sometimes competing interpretations. It is worth noting, too, that some of the more strident Republicans were left wondering just what had been gained, and what taken away, by such a gesture. As George Tucker recalled, "The expression 'we are all federalists—all republicans,' was regarded by the federalists as an overture of conciliation; but by a few of his own party, as an act of complaisance unmerited by them and unworthy of himself." In any event, virtually all those who have dwelt on the matter have agreed that the speaker was seeking to shift the plane of political commitment to something above and beyond the strictly partisan lines that had defined the contests of the 1790s.[7]

What motives and implications surrounded the phrase, however, remains unsettled. At least two general approaches to understanding the import of Jefferson's language may be discerned. One such perspective, expressed by Merrill Peterson, tends to see in these words the basis for a new and idealized conception of nationhood. Fully alive to the political dynamics to which it was responding, Peterson sees the avowal "We are all republicans, we are all federalists" as "a lofty appeal for the restoration of harmony and affection." According to Peterson, Jefferson held that "every true republican was a friend of federalism, that is, of the harmony and union of the states under the Constitution, not of the party that had corrupted this concept. The old polarities of liberty and power, rights and duties, individual enterprise and national purpose, the state and the central governments—these were swept away as the new President identified the principles of the federal union with the principles of republican freedom." Where Peterson is inclined to view Jefferson at once appealing to and recreating a new and better vision of American polity, Joseph Ellis, among others, detects a politician still very much rooted in the Manichean battles of the past decade. The very universalism remarked on by Peterson Ellis sees as evidence of glib generalization. Noting that in the author's handwritten version "federalist and republican" are not capitalized, Ellis suggests that "Jefferson was therefore referring not to the common ground shared by the two parties but to the common belief, shared by all American citizens, that a republican form of government and a federal bond among the states was most preferable. Since one would have been hard pressed to discover a handful of Americans citizens who disagreed with this observation," Ellis concludes, "his statement was more a political platitude than an ideological concession."[8]

There is of course a great deal more to Jefferson's inaugural than this single passage. I have introduced it and the diverse responses it has provoked by way of approach to the more general concern for the speech's partisan qualities. We see at once the heart of the matter: the phrase within and the speech as a whole may be read as either elevating itself and its audience above mere partisanship, or it may be viewed as a transparent bit of party grandstanding. If the former, then we have no basis for an extended treatment of the address as a party document; if the latter, then we have no basis for treating it as anything except a particularly eloquent collection of partisan platitudes. The options drawn here are no doubt reductive, but in their very starkness they may help us see more clearly that to seize upon one to the exclusion of the other is to effect an even more damaging reduction.

To reintegrate the ideal and real, the abstract and the concrete, the statesmanship and the partisanship that inhere in this text, we might invoke a set of observations applied by Professors Stanley Elkins and

Eric McKitrick. In writing of Jefferson in more general contexts, the authors note that his apparent contradictions and characteristic ambivalence "should be taken not so much as a defect" as "a distinctive quality of his mind. In charting this quality one might begin by referring to it as a "disjunction," an open space in his mental habits between the general and the particular which could sometimes assume dramatic proportions." It is in this space, this gap between "the long range and the short, and between broad conception and concrete realization" that Jefferson's address may best be placed. There we can examine the text as simultaneously elevated by principle and grounded by expedience, as both a statement on republican theory and as assisting in the practical work of political action. The burden of this section is thus not to deny the genuine reach toward the former but to first consider the partisan basis of Jefferson's masterpiece. To this end, we need to locate it at the end of a long and disruptive period in America's first decade of national existence. More specifically, we are concerned to identify eighteenth-century attitudes toward partisan politics, the unfolding dynamics of party government in the 1790s, and turn then to a more systematic examination of the text as it was informed by these developments.[9]

The Problem with Parties

In 1770 Edmund Burke published what is widely regarded as the most powerful defense of party of his time. Aiming to bolster the coalition of opposition leaders associated with the Rockingham Whigs, Burke promised to demonstrate "the ground upon which the Party stands; and how different its Constitution, as well as the persons who compose it are from the Bedfords, and Grenvilles, and other knots, who are combined for no Publick purpose; but only as a means of furthering with joint strength, their private and individual advantage." His Thoughts on the Cause of the Present Discontents set out in considerable detail not to attack parties as such, but to call for stronger, more principled party activity. In this new view, party was to be defined as "a body of men united for promoting by their joint endeavors the national interest upon some particular principle in which they are all

agreed." Here was an altogether fresh conception of associative politics, alive to the complex realities of life in opposition. The only alternative to parties, Burke argued, was acting in isolation, and in that there
could be few prospects for political action of a serious kind. "When
bad men combine," Burke concluded, "the good must associate; else
they will fall, one by one, an unpitied sacrifice in a contemptible
struggle."[10]

Burke's manifesto is worth recalling not as a representative piece of
eighteenth-century thought on the subject but as a useful contrast to
prevailing opinion. Indeed it stands virtually alone as a defense of party
at a time of nearly universal hostility—at least hostile in theory—to
such organized resistance. Where Burke saw promise for collective and
rationalized resistance to governmental forces, others discerned a deep
threat to constitutionally recognized power and public order; where
Burke found virtue in good men associating, others espied conspiratorial designs against the general welfare. Ironically, perhaps, the stream
against which he swam had been stocked not by corrupt ministerial
figures or court darlings, but by a richly funded tradition of fellow
outsiders and critics, chief among them Thomas Gordon and John
Trenchard, Viscount Bolingbroke, and David Hume. Differences aside,
they contributed significantly to the development of anti-party thought
in the eighteenth century; by turning to them for a moment, we can
better appreciate the ideological inheritance from which Jefferson drew
inspiration.

At a time when we are now more or less accustomed to the positive
role of parties in the conduct of local and national affairs, it may be
difficult to comprehend just how dangerous they were once held to be.
Antipathy to party (or "faction": the terms were frequently inter-
changed) can be traced to antiquity, but achieved its most pointed expression after the shattering events of the seventeenth century. We cannot grasp the intensity and persistence of such enmity unless we keep
in mind an axiom at the root of eighteenth-century political thought,
the notion that the state was viable only to the extent that it was unified
on a common conception of the public good. On this basis, as Gordon
Wood observes, "politics was conceived to be not the reconciling but

the transcending of the different interests of the society" as citizens pursued that good. The key to reaching such a state was to check and subordinate local, private, or mere self-interests in the service of that organic unity requisite to truly constitutional government.[11]

In a period when Englishmen were seeking to put back together the pieces of political order after the battles of the previous century, the specter of party could seem threatening indeed. It was associated, in Richard Hofstadter's summary, with "painfully deep and unbridgeable differences in national politics, with religious bigotry and clerical animus, with treason and the threat of foreign invasion, with instability and dangers to liberty." At such portentous moments in the career of the nation, parties were thus held responsible for creating discord in civil affairs, for giving to minority interests a means to despotic ends, and for polluting that fountain of all rightful government, civic virtue. This assemblage of horrors was memorably invoked by Trenchard's and Gordon's *Cato's Letters* of the early 1720s, to lasting effect both in England and later in colonial and early national America. Invariably, they argued, the enemies of constitutional government conspired to "form parties, and blow up factions to mutual animosities, that they may find protection in those animosities." In any case, Trenchard argued, "Most men are sick of party and party-leaders," and urged his readers to "exemplarily punish the parricides, and avowed enemies of all mankind."[12]

As it happened, parties and party leaders did not go away, and so the question became what to do with them. The problem with parties, in the eyes of Trenchard and Gordon, and indeed in the view of all good Whigs, was that they mobilized power independently of virtue, the one countervailing force capable of restraining their will. "It is therefore high time," wrote "Cato," "for all parties to consider what is best for the whole; and to establish such rules of communicative justice and indulgence, as may prevent oppression from any party. And this can only be done by restraining the hands of power, and fixing it within certain bounds and to its limits and expense." But could parties thus conceived ever be counted on to bend their will to the common good? Few believed it.[13]

A great deal had changed in the cultural climate in the generation after "Cato" sought to awaken readers to the evils of faction. Politics by party, however, remained as many had feared, and if the old divisions and old issues no longer defined parties in the same way, new causes and new affiliations arose to take their place and to effect the expected ends. One implausible but tempting solution to the problem was memorably penned by Bolingbroke, who in 1749 envisioned a "Patriot King," a monarch who was to "defeat the designs, and break the spirit of faction, instead of partaking in one and assuming the others." Under the circumstances, that was asking rather a good deal more than anyone had reason to expect, but in Bolingbroke's dream of a national ruler freed from the destructive pull of party he gave voice to widespread and deeply held attitudes.[14]

Now, it may seem that in Bolingbroke's idealized monarch, however ennobled, we are as yet at some remove from the republican verities of Jefferson's inaugural address. It is important to keep in mind, however, that those verities are wholly recognizable within a persistent tradition of opposition thought, indeed took their ideological power, at least in part, from that tradition. "The Americans of Jefferson's generation," Hofstadter reminds us, "had themselves been raised on imported criticisms of Walpole's era, and many of Bolingbroke's themes, the cry for a virtuous monarch, the plea that the Crown should not be the agent of a faction, above all, the attack on corruption and party—had powerful appeal to them." Thus when Bolingbroke remarked in his *Dissertation Upon Parties* that "no grief hath lain more heavily on the hearts of all good men, than those about our national divisions; about the spirit of party, which inspires animosity and breeds rancor; which hath so often destroyed our inward peace; weakened our national strength, and sullied our glory abroad," he wrote in terms deeply familiar to the disputants of Jefferson's time. The king was gone, that was true, but party was here to stay.[15]

By mid-century, indeed, the fact the factions were an intractable feature of political life was in the main conceded. Few thought that they could be actually eliminated from the scene, and increasingly the concern was not to stamp them out but to so manage parties as to mitigate their baneful effects. The challenge was compounded by the apparent fact that factions seemed to be entailed by free government; the greater the freedom of such government, the more space was opened for factions to operate. Small comfort that, thought David Hume, whose depiction of party stands as one of the most colorful and sharply edged portraits in the literature. Factions, Hume wrote in "Of Parties in General,"

> subvert government, render laws impotent, and beget the fiercest animosities among men of the same nation, who ought to give mutual assistance and protection to each other. And what should render the founders of parties more odious is the difficulty of extirpating these weeds when once they have taken root in any state. They naturally propagate themselves for many centuries, and seldom end but by the total dissolution of that government in which they are sown. They are, besides, plants which grow most plentiful in the richest soil; and though absolute governments be not wholly free from them, it must be confessed that they rise more easily and propagate themselves faster in free government, where they always infect the legislature itself, which alone could be able, by the steady application of rewards and punishments, to eradicate them.[16]

That factions grow fastest in the "richest soil" was of course a point James Madison was to treat with great dexterity in the years ahead. But for Hume and others of his time, the best to be hoped for was a system of constitutional protections against the incursion of such forces. Like "Cato" and Bolingbroke, they provided Americans with a way of talking and thinking about party that was to have discernible consequences as they set about their own task of nation-building. Again, at the heart of their shared complaint was the supposition that parties upset the natural and necessary unity upon which all vital, and certainly all genuine republican societies, were founded. When we think ahead to Jefferson's inaugural address, then, and to his subsumption of Federalism into the Republican fold, we must observe a partisan act of the most ingenious kind. As we shall discover in greater detail, he then sought not to recognize the equal claims of the opposing party, now momentarily in opposition, but to announce the triumph of a non-party, of a Republican creed that was to restore America to her original condition of unity, concord, and civic virtue.

In view of this English inheritance, it should come as no surprise that, in the words of Hofstadter, "the creators of the first American party system, on both sides, Federalists and Republicans, were men who looked upon parties as sores on the body politic." And no one looked upon those sores with greater revulsion than the one man who seemed genuinely above faction, the nation's first president. Washington's Farewell Address may well stand as the most poignant and influential attack on the evils of party in American history, a parting shot across the bow of the early republic that could not be ignored—even as it went unheeded. Washington grasped with unique clarity how fragile the great experiment in republican government remained, understood keenly Wood's point that, given "the persistence of social incoherence and change in the eighteenth century, Americans creating a new society could not conceive of the state in any other terms than organic unity." Coming as it did when it did, Washington's address was at once shaped by the party animosities of the decade and a deeply felt, indeed personal, expression of his anguish over the state of political life in the new nation. We need then to examine it briefly but in some detail, for Jefferson's inaugural address may, to an important degree, be understood as a response to his predecessor's timely lament.[17]

Washington's Farewell is perhaps best remembered for its admonition to seek with foreign nations "as little political connection as possible." On closer inspection, however, historians have shown that Washington viewed what Jefferson was to call "entangling alliances" in the more general context of party evils. As to the source, character, and effect of those evils, Washington was absolutely clear, and he aimed late in 1796 to spell them out before factional disturbances laid ruin to the republic once and for all. As with so many others of his time, the first president harkened to the days of his greatest political triumphs, when in 1788 and in 1792 it seemed that the unity of sentiment essential to free government had at length been secured. By the middle of the decade, however, that unity had been profoundly shaken by a series of domestic and foreign upheavals. Washington had naturally enough despaired over the rapid disintegration of common cause, the debased spirit that seemed to pervade the political culture. Indeed it was, as John Howe writes, "a quite remarkable phenomenon, this brutality both of expression and behavior that marked American political life with such force during these years. Involved were more than disagreements over matters of public policy—though these were real enough. For the political battles of the 1790s were grounded upon a complete distrust of the motives and integrity, the honesty and intentions of one's political opponents." This much George Washington could not abide.[18]

At the well springs of this national unhappiness was to be found party, that familiar but insidious enemy to all free government. The logic of Washington's attack on it was based on a principle of great simplicity but of great weight: "The very idea of the power and the right of the people to establish government presupposes the duty of every individual to obey the established government." Anything and anyone seeking to disrupt the processes necessary to the function of that government was therefore to be protected against with the greatest possible vigilance. Combinations of citizens whose design it was to check the proper execution of the laws, of which parties were a type, were "destructive of this fundamental principle, and of fatal tendency." The factions produced by such forces may now and then prove expedient in gaining the people's favor, Washington reasoned. But in the long run they were more likely "to become potent engines, by which cunning, ambitious, and unprincipled men will be enabled to subvert the power of the people and to usurp for themselves the reins of government, destroying afterwards the very engines which have lifted them to unjust dominion."[19]

Like most who reflected on the matter, Washington acknowledged that the tendency to such associations was probably fated, "inseparable from our nature, having its root in the strongest passions of the human mind." Faction was evident in governments of all kinds, everywhere and apparently forever. Its effects were most damaging, most tragic, in popular republics, where the straightest line from disorder to despotism was drawn by party dissension. The catalogue of mischiefs was truly impressive: the spirit of party served to "distract the public councils," "enfeeble the public administration," "agitates the community with ill-founded jealousies and false alarms," "kindles the animosity of one part against the other," "foments occasionally riot and insurrection," and "opens the door to foreign influence and corruption." But for all that, there could be no excuse for failing to resist such effects, for the future of republican government remained at stake. Given this "constant danger of excess," Washington warned, "the effort ought to be by force of public opinion, to mitigate and assuage it. A fire not to be quenched, it demands a uniform vigilance to prevent its bursting into a flame, lest, instead of warming, it should consume."[20]

In such language George Washington, America's version of Bolingbroke's idealized "Patriot King," blasted those forces which threatened to reduce republican government into partisan squabbling. The attack was severe, and it was heart-felt, but we must again recognize in it an irony to which we have already been introduced. Washington's address was itself a party act, the words of a leader who came to office above the fray but unable to stay there, a critic of opposition, resentful of those who would express their own resentments against administrative measures. By mid-decade the president was firmly attached, in the public mind at least, to the Federalist persuasion, and though he would claim otherwise, Washington had himself become a party man, a leading player in the disputes which so inflamed the political landscape. It was true, as Hofstadter has written, that "his intellectual confusion about the problem of government and opposition was altogether genuine, and that it partook of an intellectual difficulty quite common among his contemporaries." But common or not, Washington's "confusion" was enshrined by the Olympian pronouncements of the Farewell Address, where he gave to anti-party sentiment its most partisan, its most eloquent voice. His administrations had been subject to years of mounting displeasure, he had himself been criticized in the Republican press, and he knew that his legacy was vulnerable in ways not dreamed of before assuming office. Thus struggling to redeem his leadership and his nation, he could not, in the end, separate concerted opposition from a conception of party as destructive to republican government.[21]

Neither, it may plausibly be argued, could Thomas Jefferson. He was, of course, a leading figure in precisely that culture of opposition which so dismayed Washington, and he stands as the centerpiece of what Joyce Appleby has characterized as "the first truly American political movement." Indeed for one who complained of being "a constant butt of every shaft of calumny which malice and falsehood could form, and the presses, public speakers, or private letters disseminate," Jefferson had proved adept at placing himself in the crossfire of public debate. In one way or another, the Virginian figured in the vitriolic contest over Hamilton's financial program, materially supported a heated partisan newspaper war, pilloried "Monocratic" Federalist leaders, and penned the openly divisive Kentucky Resolutions of 1798. This was not a man who, for all his protestations to the contrary, shrank from the political battle for the hearts and minds of the new republic. As early as late 1792, Lance Banning demonstrates, "a set of fears and expectations that had prompted objections to administration plans since the first days of the government had come together in an integrated whole. This systematic ideology," Banning concludes, "was both a product and a cause of the emergence of the first political party of the modern sort." From the beginning and throughout the early stages of this ideology can be discerned the hand of one who had declared that if he had to go to heaven with a party, he "would not go there at all."[22]

Jefferson's professions and his action, then, cannot help but invite pointed questions as to what he actually thought about the role of party in the conduct of political life. We may at a minimum observe that he shared with Washington a complex but not fully coherent vision of a nation bound by a common set of convictions, and that he saw his efforts, as Washington saw his own, as a struggle to restore the country to a state of primal integrity. He was in this sense the leader of a "proto-party," in James Roger Sharp's phrasing, a group "not seen by the participants as a vehicle for reconciling differences but rather as a means of organizing and mobilizing public opinion to form a national consensus and political hegemony based upon a particular ideological perspective." When Jefferson wrote and spoke about parties, then, we must be mindful that he did so from a set of assumptions quite different from our own. There is some truth, to be sure, in David Mayer's claim that Jefferson "justified his partisan activities as being in the public interest but was unwilling to acknowledge the same motives in his political foes." At the same time, it remained altogether unclear to many how, given the principle of "organic unity" to which Wood alludes, one might recognize legitimate opposition in the form of partisan loyalty. This dilemma is very much in evidence in Jefferson's first inaugural address, and as we approach its analysis it will prove useful to review what he had to say when he considered the problem with parties.[23]

Perhaps the most direct, though no doubt simplified, way of putting the point is this: *we* can see in Jefferson's actions the spirit of party—he did not. And the reason is not owing to blindness or to self-deception, but to a vision of government and the nation as a whole as essentially, already *republican*. From this view, to which he gave expression time and again through the decade preceding his address, Jefferson saw party as a momentary distortion, an unfortunate but doomed attempt to delude the people into anti-republican measures. Party, to put it colloquially, was what *they* did, the Federalists, the "Anglo-men," the "Monocrats," and the entire "reign of witches" that had seized only temporary control of political affairs. But Jefferson's optimism, so frequently remarked upon, truly was unbounded, and never more so than when he reflected on the capacity of his countrymen to embrace finally the gift of republican government. True, this return to common sense required the leadership of a vigilant elite, but in this, too, Jefferson had complete confidence. He could thus be as alarmed as any democrat about the incursions of monarchical sentiment into the national host, but there was for Jefferson an almost foreordained guarantee that the people, the republican nation, would prevail. "I know that there are some among us," he wrote James Madison in 1789, "who would now establish a monarchy. But they are inconsiderable in number and weight of character. The rising race are all republicans. We were educated in royalism; no wonder if some of us retain that idolatry still. Our young people are educated in republicanism," Jefferson concluded with typi-

cal sanguinity, and so any "apostasy from that to royalism is unprecedented and impossible."[24]

The years ahead were to test such optimism severely. Factional discord on the order of the 1790s could not be dismissed as anything except a deep tear in the fabric of national unity, and even one so convinced of the people's essentially republican virtue as Jefferson could
not ignore the peril thus posed. If nothing else, party strife had the effect
of drawing the lines of loyalty in clear, indeed stark terms. "Pushed to
expose the assumptions in each others' positions," Appleby notes, "the
Federalists and the Jeffersonians made brilliantly clear that the character of America's future was at issue." Jefferson never abandoned his
conviction that the opponents of republican government were but a
disaffected minority of would-be monarchists, but he eventually conceded that the grounds of debate had been deeply inscribed. One had
to make a choice. "[W]here the principle of difference is as substantial
and as strongly pronounced as between the republican and the
Monocrats of our country," he confided to William Branch Giles, "I hold
it as honorable to take a firm and decided part, and as immoral to pursue a middle line, as between the practices of honest men, and rogues,
into which every country is divided."[25]

Here then we have a key to Jefferson's sense of what party entailed
as a political reality. It was not so much a matter, as we might now think
of it, as a contest between two equally legitimate aspirants to political
power, Federalists and Republicans, each vying for votes in the way
Democrats and Republicans might in our day. It was rather a
Manichean battle between "honest men" and "rogues," those who
sought to make good on the promises of the Revolution and those who
would subvert its cherished ends. Still, through it all, through the en-
trenchment of Hamiltonian policy, through the hated Jay Treaty of
1795–96, even through the pernicious Alien and Sedition Acts of 1798,
Jefferson remained convinced that republicanism, not party, was sure
to prevail. Federalist measures, to be certain, had unleashed fearsome
and destructive energies, but there could be no just reason for coun-
sels of disunion. "A little patience," Jefferson advised John Taylor of
Caroline, "and we shall see the reign of witches pass over, their spells

dissolve, and the people, recovering their true sight, restore their government to it's [sic] true principles." By decade's end, as Jefferson was contemplating his own assumption to office, this basic optimism remained firm. "The unquestionable republicanism of the American mind," he assured Elbridge Gerry, "will break through the mist under which it has been clouded, and will oblige it's [sic] agents to reform the principles and practices of their administration."[26]

Partisan Dynamics in the First Inaugural Address

If Jefferson cared to look for further evidence of such "unquestionable republicanism," he need not have looked far nor waited long. News of his election spread quickly, and was met for the most part with a heartening combination of relief, revelry, and abundant good will. Not that both parties were above rubbing it in a little. The new president's most avid supporters went to elaborate lengths to celebrate the great event, perhaps none so imaginatively as the organizers of a pageant exhibited in his home state. "A beautiful virgin" mocked vanquished Federalists by proclaiming "Liberty at the point of Death," while figures surrounding her—a priest, a statesmen, an orator—advised the "irresolute and amazed" crowd to "exchange your absurd equality of rights, for the beautiful equality of balances." In western Pennsylvania, Federalist sympathizers told of a republican party "at the house of Jesse Hart," where the celebrants were observed to "erect a whiskey alias sedition pole," and, "after performing many Indian dances, and singing the favorite Jacobin songs," they at length "took a very plentiful dole of the juice of the grain, and reeled home to recount to their wives and children, at the wonderful exploits of the day." The presumably more sober citizens of Philadelphia celebrated with equal vigor. "A procession was formed," readers learned, "which is stated, for splendor and extent, to have surpassed any thing of the kind excepting the procession of 1787." Parades, prayers, a reading of the Declaration of Independence, music and oratory, artillery discharges, ringing bells, and ships in full dress-withal, reported the *National Intelligencer,* a happy day indeed, when even "the federal prints, with commendable candour, state the arrangements made to this effect, to have been executed with complete success."[27]

No matter their party allegiances, citizens of the early republic could not have helped but to acknowledge how pervasive, how entrenched and damaging party animosities had been to the political culture of the time. Jefferson's first inaugural address, by contrast, seemed conspicuously mild in tone, temper, and profession of principle. A new day, it appeared, truly was at hand. Even veteran critics like Joseph Hale, writing to Rufus King from Boston, conceded that "no man ever entered upon the administration of a free government under more favorable auspices than Mr. Jefferson." To Robert Goodloe Harper, as staunch a Federalist as might be found among Jefferson's opponents, an eery calm seemed to have settled over the typically bumptious capital city. The president's address, observed the North Carolinian, "was well calculated to inspire these sentiments and to afford the hope of such an administration as may conduce to his own glory and the public good. Before the evening, all was quiet as if no change had taken place." The "sentiments" to which Harper alluded—love of country, commitment to the constitution, republican freedom, and national prosperity—were felt everywhere to have captured all right-thinking Americans. "With these maxims," DuPont de Nemour wrote the president from France, "you will enchant one half of the human race, and finally the other half."[28]

No one was as alive to the auspiciousness of the moment as the speaker himself. Jefferson was fully aware that the words he spoke on March 4 must appear at once conciliatory and forceful, conscious of the circumstances from which they arose but not merely determined by those circumstances. Above all, the first inaugural address had to assure his fellow citizens that not party but republicanism had triumphed. It was in this sense a speech of vindication, but not for that reason vindictive; a speech of victory, yes, but not of conquerors and conquered. In the end, Jefferson understood that what had just transpired was the supreme test of the great experiment, and his relief as well as his pride was unbounded. "The storm through which we have passed," he wrote to his old friend John Dickinson, "has been tremendous indeed. The tough sides of our argosie have been thoroughly tried. Her strength has stood the waves into which she was steered with a view to sink her. We shall put her on her republican tack," he vowed two days after the inaugural address, "and she will now show by the beauty of her motion, the skill of her builders." All the good will palpably surrounding Jefferson's election and inaugural, of course, could not eliminate all those who would persist in steering the ship of state into dangerous waters. But here too the president remained optimistic, if not overly so. Nevertheless, he confided to James Monroe, "I am in hopes my inaugural address . . . will present the leading objects to be conciliation and adherence to sound principle. This I know to be impracticable with the leaders of the late faction," but these high Federalists he promised to "abandon as incurables, and will never turn an inch out of my way to reconcile them. But with the main body of the federalists I believe it is very practicable."[29]

Again we spy the key to opening up our reading of Jefferson's first inaugural address in its partisan guise. The president very clearly and very early reasoned that the factional pressures which had distorted the shape of republican government could be alleviated; this was to be effected, however, not by dissuading the Federalist leadership but by isolating them, by deploying the rhetorical power inherent in republicanism to recall the people back from their momentary delusion. To gain full appreciation of the difficulty and stakes involved in this battle, however, we need to remind ourselves of just how precarious was the political situation at the time of Jefferson's ascent to the executive office. The reason so many marveled at the calm after his election was that so little was calm before it. Without rehearsing in any great detail the complexities of that election, we can with a brief review enhance our perspective on Jefferson's speech and its partisan implications.

Owing to a constitutional oversight, corrected finally by the Twelfth Amendment in 1804, ballots did not distinguish between the offices of president and vice president. Whomever received the most votes was thereby elected to the higher office. Thus Jefferson, receiving fewer votes than John Adams in 1796, was elected vice president. In 1800, Jefferson and his "running mate" Aaron Burr each received seventy-three electoral votes, with Adams commanding sixty-five, Pinckney sixty-four, and John Jay one. In the event, the tie was slated to be resolved by vote in the House of Representatives. Federalist intransigence and Burr's reluctance to remove himself from consideration created a national as well as constitutional crisis. Jefferson was certain that "time has been given to the states to recover from the temporary frenzy into which they had been decoyed, to rally round the constitution, and to rescue it from the destruction with which it had been threatened even at our own hands." After a protracted period of wrangling, including threats of disunion, cajoling, backroom deals, and complicated maneuvering, Jefferson was finally elected president on the 16th ballot on February 17, 1801. In retrospect, we are inclined perhaps to conclude that a technical glitch in the electoral process had merely disrupted an otherwise workable system, and that, in any case, things turned out well and as expected. At the time, however, few took so benign a view of the matter, and many despaired for the prospects of the nation itself. "The newness of the nation," contends the historian James Roger Sharp, "the fragility of its institutions, and the depth of the hostility and suspicion all contributed to the creation of a volatile situation in which the union's continued existence became highly problematic." No seaman, Jefferson knew that he and the nation as a whole had been through a tremendous storm indeed.[30]

Advancing closer now to the text of Jefferson's address, we are in a position to state more clearly what is meant by its partisan ambitions. A speech may be viewed as partisan to the extent that it gives generalized expression to a particular ideological perspective; that it addresses points at issue; and that it seeks to transform those points by rendering them non-controversial by redefining them not as objects of contest but as principles authorized by consensus. This is a rather abstract way of putting it, perhaps, but it allows us to see up close what is at work when Jefferson says what he says and how. This process is most clearly marked in the inaugural address by the speaker's effort to re-align key terms and relationships in such a way that the ground from under the opposition is eliminated as a source of legitimate opposition. Here this work can be observed in a manner wholly consistent with Jefferson's comment to Monroe about Federalist "incurables" and "the main body of the federalists," whom he sought to call back to the fold. The speech in this sense works to secure the blessings of victory by bracketing out the leadership and inviting (or absorbing) the rest into a unified structure of republican principles. The conciliatory function of the address is thus more strategic, more ideologically cunning, than is frequently acknowledged. If it was conciliatory, as Hofstadter argues, it was "not a way of arriving at coexistence or of accommodating a two-party system, but a technique of absorption: he proposed to win over the major part of the amenable Federalists, leaving the intractables an impotent minority faction rather than a full-fledged opposition party." Jefferson's strategy, Hofstadter concludes, aimed "at a party to end parties" and so "formed another chapter in the quest for unanimity."[31]

Such a strategy may be seen operating in three distinct but obviously related ways in the second and third paragraphs of the written text. These sections give rich evidence of Jefferson's skill in simultaneously identifying his principles with those of republicanism and his audience, even as he construes the posture of his critics as unacceptable to those principles. In the first instance, he artfully depicts "the contest of opinion" through which the nation had just emerged in both positive and negative terms: positively, the better to subsume public debate under the auspices of republican virtue; negatively, the better to segregate those who seek to persist in lost, past, and damaging causes. In the second instance, we see Jefferson's focus on "wise and frugal government" as appealing to a providential Americanism, where resistance to his republican vision is to be taken as resistance to both God and God's nature. Each of these paragraphs and the partisan functions they are made to serve will be examined in greater detail as follows.

"THE CONTEST OF OPINION"

For a man who had spent the last decade decrying the effects of party on the political life of the nation, it may well seem odd that Jefferson chose now to speak so blithely of a mere "contest of opinion." Little in this passage, nor of the address as a whole, suggests anything of the deep anxiety over faction so evident in Washington's Farewell, and we might wonder whether Jefferson was, not altogether ingenuously, glossing the problem to make it disappear. If nothing else, such euphemistic language could serve to deflect attention away from the speaker's own role in the "contest," a possibility not lost on his embittered critics. To the *Gazette of the United States,* Jefferson's words appeared "to have been dictated by a heart glowing with a generous ardor for his country's welfare, and tender concern for her fatal differentiation." That said, however, "gloomy doubts have already arisen as to the sincerity of the professions of Mr. Jefferson."[32]

In view of the context and of the inaugural address's general purposes, however, we need not doubt that Jefferson was anything except sincere. The nation had, after all, survived—indeed grown and prospered—through the decade, and now here was a duly elected chief executive whose very identity was a product of opposition politics. This much is not to suggest rosy naivete: far from it. By depicting partisan strife as a "contest of opinion," Jefferson was in effect announcing that the nation had in fact come of age, that it had been tested in the crucible of public debate and emerged stronger as a result. If we pay close attention to the meaning and force of these lines, we glimpse an early expression of a theme that will run throughout the address. The key here is to recognize what might be called the rhetorical direction of Jefferson's reasoning, his way of characterizing a certain movement from one state of political affairs to another, a movement always forward, always toward a greater realization of the republican experiment.

This movement is most evident in a temporal shift from past to present, from division to unity, and from appearance to essence. In each case, we observe a subtle but strategic argument that republicanism has been fully revealed to be capable of withstanding and finally triumphing over forces that once threatened its very existence. From the vantage point of 1801, the contentions of the past had been evidence not of a battle or war, but of "contention," not destructive polemics but animated discussion. From this perspective, moreover, Americans could even take pride that, however difficult the period of trial may have been, in the end republican faith in free speech and thought had been fully vindicated. It is crucial to our understanding of this particular logic that we note in Jefferson's language the temporal shifts marking this process. The contest of opinion shaping past events is made just that— a past fact. Now, Jefferson stresses, the great issue has been "decided by the voice of the nation, announced according to the rules of the Constitution," and now, therefore, "all will, of course, arrange themselves under the will of the law, and unite in common efforts for the common good." The seemingly innocuous phrase, "of course," is actually central to the meaning and power of Jefferson's point. A quarter of a century earlier, Jefferson had appealed to "the course of human events" to accord the Revolution the status of a necessity, a necessity, as Stephen Lucas explains, "as inescapable, as inevitable, as unavoidable within the course of human events as the motions of the tides or the changing of the seasons within the course of natural events." Similarly, in 1801 Jefferson announced to his readers and listeners that they were victors in this, America's second revolution. The contest of opinion had perhaps been inevitable, and it may have strengthened the sinews of a young nation, but the point here is that it was now history, in the past, for all intents and purposes an artifact of a recent but bygone age. Its passing, implies Jefferson, is worthy of comment only as proof of the new nation's claim to the future.[33]

The second key movement conducted by Jefferson's language may be observed as a shift from a condition of difference to that of unity. Clearly related to the temporal development we have just noted, this process again reinforces the positive construction the speaker places on what might otherwise be cause for lament. The election of 1800, for all its animus and confusion, Jefferson held to be a revolution as important as that of 1776. It announced not the emergence but the success of republican government, and that fact portended immediately all the new president's most cherished hopes. "I hope to see shortly a perfect consolidation," he informed John Dickinson, "to effect which, nothing shall be spared on my part. A just and solid republican government maintained here, will be a standing monument and example for the aim and imitation of the people of other countries."[34]

The boast of republicanism, indeed the very precondition of its success in America and the world, was that it could effectively govern a free people without thereby diminishing their liberties as a free people. True, as Madison in Federalist #10 and many others admitted, free peoples in large republics were notoriously inclined to act rather too freely, to break into factions or to pursue their self interests to the detriment of the common good. But America in 1801 had shown the world that this was not inevitably so, that a diverse and expansive republic could gather under a single republican system of government. And the reason for this success was that virtue, that collective commitment to the common good, was thought to reside in the breast of every true American. Indeed, Jefferson wrote to Joseph Priestly shortly after his inauguration, "The order and good sense displayed in this recovery from delusion, and in the momentous crisis which lately arose, really bespeak a strength of character in our nation which augurs well for the duration of our Republic; and I am much better satisfied now of it's [sic] stability than I was before it was tried." The "strength of character" to which Jefferson refers was precisely that ability and willingness to unite in the face of debilitating division. Virtue in this sense, however broadly or vaguely understood, had little room and less time for sustained contests of opinion. It rather represented the motive force and fullest realization of the human potential for collective self-government in a polity united by a shared commitment to equal rights for all citizens.[35]

We have so far identified in Jefferson's speech two thematic shifts that characterize his response to partisan conflict. A third movement complements and extends upon these relationships—from past to present, from difference to unity—by posing a disjunctive relationship between appearance and essence. In this case the distinction was less philosophical than political, a way of calculating what signified what, how much weight ought to be assigned to particular issue, how to make sense of competing voices, rival views, sharp criticism. Pessimists could reflect on the events of the past decade and plausibly ask whether the new nation was in effect a new Babel. Under such circumstances, what were the options? To condone seemed irresponsible, to silence, despotic. But here again republican virtue could be appealed to as way out of the dilemma. Virtue taken in this sense contained a principle of reason, a capacity for discernment and prudential judgment that helped to resolve just these kinds of problems. This was why Jefferson was adamant when it came to protecting rights of expression, why he announced to Elbridge Gerry that he was "against all the violations of the constitution to silence by force and not reason the complaints of criticisms, just or unjust, of our citizens against the conduct of their agents," and swore to Benjamin Rush, "upon the altar of god, eternal hostility against every form of tyranny over the mind of man."[36]

Reason unfettered, Jefferson believed, naturally inclined itself toward considerations of the common good. And when it was thus exercised, thus trained upon the scenes of political life, it proved fully up to the task of distinguishing between appearances and essences. The inaugural address pretends to no systematic treatment of the point; Jefferson's was a political task requiring rhetorical skill, and he appealed to the role of reason as a way of authorizing a particular interpretation of events. To that end, we have seen, he characterizes partisan strife as a contest of opinion only, of aspects worn and mistaken strangers. If we look more closely at the balance of the paragraph, we see that it is largely structured around this disjunction, where difference and conflict are consigned to the realm of opinion, identity of interests and civil harmony to principle. Reason, what we might call republican reason, comes into play as it recognizes the difference between these two realms and resists confusing them. Appealing to his audience to "unite with one heart and one mind," Jefferson proceeds to deliver his memorable evocation of the national self-image. It bears quotation in full:

During the throes and convulsions of the ancient world, during the agonizing spasms of infuriated man, seeking through blood and slaughter his long-lost liberty, it was not wonderful that agitation of the billows should reach even this distant and peaceful shore; that this should be more felt and feared by some and less by others, and should divide opinions as to measures of safety. But every difference of opinion is not a difference of principle. We have called by different names brethren of the same principle. We are all Republicans, we are all Federalists. If there be any among us who would wish to dissolve this Union or to change its republican form, let them stand undisturbed as monuments of the safety with which error of opinion may be tolerated where reason is left free to combat it.

Here is perhaps our finest expression of faith in republican government. But it is also an expression of faith in republicanism's capacity to absorb dissent—not by indulging and certainly not by encouraging it, but by properly ascertaining its status and relationship to the essential principles binding the nation together. Still, and here we turn toward the other side of Jefferson's coin, we cannot help but note the implication that dissent from these principles can only be "errors of opinion," to be tolerated as befits a free people—but to be combated as well.

As with so many dimensions of this address, Jefferson's language admits of several interpretations; in this case, we find reason to ask twice about the "contest of opinion" animating the political culture of his time. In one reading, as previously suggested, we find a relatively benign rendering, where republican virtue is pronounced strong enough to have withstood such dissent and ultimately to have absorbed it into a greater and unified whole. On this view, Jefferson is the consummate statesman, extending an olive branch to his opponents and beckoning Americans of all persuasions to a single republican standard. Here Jefferson's image is firmly impressed on the historical imagination. A second look at the paragraph, however, reveals something more at work in Jefferson's own imagination, a way of seeing and shaping events that is more pointed, more aggressively partisan than our first reading might suggest. If in the former interpretation dissent was absorbed into the fabric of republicanism, here it is characterized in such a manner as to raise questions about the prospects of opposition as such. While we must be careful not to overstate the point, Jefferson's inaugural speech, and this paragraph especially, gives evidence that it was written by a man whose resentments, anxieties, and uncertainties about partisan politics had not simply disappeared into the crisp March air.

The quickest way to the point is to ask how Jefferson actually characterizes political opposition. In part, as we have seen, he diminishes any threat by remanding it to the past, to the fleeting differences of opinion through which a republican people must travel. This, let us say, is the optimistic Jefferson. But if we submit the text to closer scrutiny, we find that he takes a very dim view of opposition indeed, so dim in fact that in the end we might be excused for not being able to distinguish between a "contest of opinion" and treason itself. Here is a rather more pessimistic Jefferson, whose art of depiction is particularly evident in the broad strokes with which he paints the motives, means, and effects of political dissent. The rhetorical force of this art is achieved through its implicit association of such dissent with the extremes of political unrest; those who remain opposed to the government, accordingly, must either concede or stand exposed as enemies to the republican peace.

So we may ask again: when opposition is invoked in this paragraph, what is it made to look like? Where does it come from and what does it do? What kind of people act this way, what are the consequences of such actions, and what responses are appropriate? Without implicating his opponents directly or by name, Jefferson consistently places them in the company of forces alien to the American experiment. Those unsympathetic to the give and take of political debate—and we again recall that Jefferson had been the de facto leader of the opposition for much of the decade—are "strangers," outsiders who are "unused to think freely and to speak and to write what they think." By an ingenious twist of reasoning, the speaker transforms that tolerance for strife into a vestige of a past that must be overcome, where social unrest is replaced through the restoration of social equilibrium, that "harmony and affection without which liberty and even life itself are but dreary things." Such a return to natural republican order had been severely disrupted, of course, by the notorious Alien and Sedition Acts only a few years ago, and Jefferson is quick now to strike a parallel between those measures and the repressive religious battles of a world far away. He thus asks his audience to reflect that, "having banished from our land that religious intolerance under which mankind so long bled and

suffered, we have yet gained little if we countenance a political intolerance as despotic, as wicked, and capable of as bitter and bloody persecutions."

Such supporters of the despised acts as may have been in attendance
no doubt blanched at the association of their efforts to stabilize the early
republic with the wars of Europe, but for Jefferson at least the analogy
was all but self-evident. Accordingly, the claim that all true patriots were
both federalists and republicans takes on a rather more decisive meaning. Those who would resist the identification, those who would continue to count themselves out of the new order, could no longer appeal
to the standard of legitimate opposition. The logic is clearly disjunctive: either one willingly acceded to the Jeffersonian persuasion, or one
relinquished title to republican citizenship. "If there be any among us
who would wish to dissolve this Union or to change its republican form,"
Jefferson declares, "let them stand undisturbed as monuments of the
safety with which error of opinion may be tolerated where reason is
left free to combat it." Through the centuries, this sentiment, so exquisitely rendered, has rightfully been recognized as a hallmark of liberal
thought; it is thus difficult to recapture the force of its practical implications. As admirably idealized as the phrase may be, it nevertheless
effects a complete separation of the "we" and the "they," the victors from
the vanquished. Those persisting in their folly are to be taken as "monuments" only, mute and archaic remains to be tolerated, undisturbed
reminders of what might have been.

Chief among Federalist fears for the new nation was that, as a republic, America could never assume sufficient strength to maintain
itself. It had rather to be worked at, achieved through a complex and
aggressive process of consolidation. This anxiety dated to the very in-
ception of the republic, and it drove the machinery of Hamiltonian
policy throughout the 1790s. Jefferson shared a concern that the people
might become complacent, but he sought now in his moment of triumph to place these consolidationists as enemies not only of Republicans but republicanism itself. "I know, indeed, that some honest men
fear that a republican government can not be strong, that this Government is not strong enough," he explains, but (and here we note the

semantic shift) "would the honest patriot, in the full tide of successful experiment, abandon a government which has so far kept us free and firm on the theoretic and visionary fear that this Government, the world's best hope, may by possibility want energy to preserve itself? I trust not." By implication, those who grant no such trust are in fact not honest patriots at all. They would abandon this, the "world's best hope," and for that Jefferson could never forgive his Federalist critics. Arrogating to themselves the power rightfully vested in the people, they had demanded a trust that could never be returned. History itself revealed that they pretended to be "angels in the forms of kings" who, in the end, were neither.

By a subtle process of transference, then, we see Jefferson at once conveying an attitude of benign tolerance for opposition politics even as he covers that politics with the cloak of illegitimacy. Such associative guilt colors those outside the pale of the new administration as "strangers," "dreary," given to despotic and wicked intolerance, at best monuments, at worst pretentious visionaries who would assume false title to a nation they nearly let slip through their disloyal and untrusting hands. Here is the other angle of Jefferson's vision, seen not as opposed to his more positive view but filling it out, expanding and complicating his understanding of what was truly at stake in the "revolution of 1800."

"A CHOSEN COUNTRY"

Looking back over the first months of Jefferson's presidency, Connecticut Federalist Roger Griswold could only despair. "Under this administration nothing is to remain as it was," he wrote, where seemingly "every minutia is to be changed. When Mr. Adams was President, the door of the president's House opened to the East. Mr. Jefferson has closed that door and opened a new door to the West." Embittered it may have been, but Griswold's point was sharply observed and, as events were to play themselves out in the next several years, prescient enough. Literally and figuratively, Jefferson appeared to many as having turned his eyes away from the old and toward a new land, an America whose geographic horizons offered a perfect complement to the expansive vistas of republican government. No other inaugural address, perhaps no other speech in American history, gives such poignant and positive expression to this sense of bounty; for the first time ever, it seemed, a people, a land, and a political order had been perfectly synchronized. Here was evidence if any were needed that America was indeed "a chosen country," as Jefferson put it, and in thus speaking to its prospects he took the first step, in the words of Peter Onuf, toward "an exultant leap into futurity for a people who had barely survived the transit from the first generation to the second."[37]

Congressman Griswold's lament, however, reminds us again that for all of Jefferson's optimism, for all of his hopes that Americans would take that leap together and at once, he yet faced the remnants of a bitterly divisive struggle. The paragraph previously quoted, the inaugural's third, consists of three sentences only, but it gives us ample evidence for observing in a second sense how the speech is made to serve partisan purposes. Where we have seen in the first instance how Jefferson simultaneously absorbs and segregates political opposition, we discover here a similar but distinctive effort to eliminate Federalism from the text of the republican creed. The partisan work of the paragraph is to so pronounce a set of principles that by direct implication any opposition to them constitutes a failure of patriotic faith. We have in these few sentences, then, a complex and formally integrated statement of that creed, at once expressing the speaker's soaring aspirations and establishing a conception of rights against which Federalist actions must be viewed as a violation of republicanism itself.

We will identify and examine those rights in greater detail shortly, but for now it is worth noting the overall organization and development of this key paragraph. Recalling that the previous paragraph unfolded *temporally* from past to future, we find here a set of *spatial* images that give structure and meaning to Jefferson's language. The distinction is neither incidental nor small; indeed it is central to the economy of the text as a whole. At this level of organization, the paragraph may be viewed in two phases, the first registering an ever-expanding vision of America, her land, and people, the second delimiting the scope and function of the government through which that vision is to be mediated. This play of expansion and delimitation represents the formal achievement of the paragraph, but it is basic to the argument itself. Jefferson's aim is to establish a radically different conception of what it was that grounded and justified the republican experiment; to this end, he insisted that pride of place be given not to government, but to the people—hence the celebration of America as a "chosen country" and the concomitant restriction of centralized government. The eminent Jefferson scholar Joseph Ellis states the point forcefully: "the truly creative transformation, again more implied than asserted, was Jefferson's suggestion that the true, indeed only source of energy in a republic was not the government per se but the voluntary popular opinion on which it rested. The traditional assumption, which was a bedrock conviction among all Federalists, was that an active federal government was necessary to embody authority and focus national policy." By contrast, Ellis concludes, "[T]he Jeffersonian mentality by-passed such traditional concerns and celebrated the ideal of liberation. Lurking in his language about what makes a republican government strong was a belief in the inherent coherence of an American society that did not require the mechanisms of the state to maintain national stability."[38]

The paragraph may thus be taken as a prose equivalent to an expanding circle, where the principle of growth is made to apply to the people, the principle of delimitation to government. At the center of this circle Jefferson locates a pair of sources—nature and providence—at the heart of republican authority. Underwriting them all, indeed providing the basis for that "inherent coherence of an American society" Ellis mentions, is an appeal to human rights, especially as they bear on considerations of autonomy, labor, and esteem. These rights, we shall see, function not only as the foundation of Jefferson's thought, but implicitly as the objects of Federalist depredations. They serve accordingly as a positive rationale for republican government *and* as a negative injunction against those who would disrupt its favored prospects.

Jefferson begins by assuming what had earlier required assertion: that the people were bound in a common commitment to both "Federalist and Republic principles," to both "union and representative government." The weight and force of this sentence is a function not of its nouns, so to speak, but of its verbs and adjectives; Jefferson appeals to his audience to harness these principles to the active will of the people, hence to pursue them with "courage and confidence." The recurrent use of the pronominal "our" (nine times in the paragraph) reinforces further the sense of collective agency to which the speaker appeals. Having thus established a common and active identity, Jefferson turns to elaborating the distinctive characteristics of that identity. It is telling that the first such distinction marks what Americans are *not*—that is, not European, not subject to the "throes and convulsions of the ancient world" mentioned in the previous paragraph. Americans are rather "kindly separated by nature and a wide ocean from the exterminating havoc of one quarter of the globe; possessing a chosen country, with room enough for our descendants to the thousandth and thousandth generation." More than one historian has observed in these words a "breathtaking hyperbole," but in fact the sentiment is familiar to the Jeffersonian creed. As Peter Onuf explains, "[T]he consciousness of one generation giving way to the next suggested an organic, quasi-familial conception of the nation. Over time," Onuf concludes, "the thickening weave of family connection, interdependent interest, and affectionate fellow feeling would provide rich soil for raising young patriots." The line between hyperbole and optimism, always thin, is here used to push back the horizons of nationhood.[39]

Who are these heirs to a country so chosen? Jefferson's answer comes in the form of a series of attributions, the aggregation of which constitutes as flattering a portrait of the American character as any citizen could wish. It is here, importantly, that Jefferson introduces his view of the people as a rights-bearing people; Americans in this sense are seen not merely as having rights, but as being defined by them. They are Americans, that is, *because* they literally embody such rights as basic to their shared identity. Together these rights, as I have suggested, form the conceptual center of this paragraph and so invite closer scrutiny. The first to which Jefferson refers is "our equal right to the use of our own faculties." What is the source and authority of this right, this freedom of conscience and its attendant claims to autonomy? The paragraph is structured, we recall, by appeal to three forms of moral sovereignty—nature, providence, and government—and it is in the first of these that we find our answer. As nature had so kindly separated American from their European forebears, so it has bestowed upon them a natural right to "the use of our own faculties," as it has the right "to the acquisition of our own industry," as well as "to honor and confidence from our fellow-citizens." By thus locating the source and authority of these three rights—to self, to labor, to esteem—Jefferson in effect withholds them from the realm of the contingent; they were to be considered not the products of a given political order or gift of government, but the very well springs of the people's identity.

Abstracted from their context these sentiments would appear so unassailable as to be truistic. What good American, what genuine republican, would dare say otherwise? But we know of course that the first inaugural address was very much a performance born of a particular time and place, very much the product of someone who had triumphed through a period of intense political rivalry. Returned to their context, Jefferson's rights take on an implicit but unmistakably partisan flavor. As the author of the Kentucky Resolutions, he had with Madison led the fight against the Federalist-inspired Alien and Sedition Acts, the intent of which was to bring the full force of law against those who exercised rights of expression against the reigning administration. As the chief voice of opposition to Hamilton's economic policy, Jefferson had sought to check government's claim on the product of free labor; and as the object of venomous public attacks he had suffered as no candidate had ever before the calumny of the Federalist press. Without having to say so explicitly, Jefferson posed his conception of natural rights as a way of reasserting the priority of self, labor, and esteem over and against such foes to republican virtue.

The characteristic blend of idealism and partisanship we see at work in Jefferson's comments on natural rights we see in his reference to religion also. As a chosen people, Jefferson intoned, Americans were blessed by providence as well as by nature. Here was a nation "enlightened by a benign religion, professed, indeed, and practiced in various forms," but a faith that in different ways delivered "honesty, truth, temperance, gratitude, and the love of man." All Americans, he continued, recognized in different ways "an overruling Providence, which by all its dispensations proves that it delights in the happiness of man here and his greater happiness hereafter." Jefferson, of course, had weathered many years of abuse on the score of his religion—or, as his critics insisted, lack thereof. The campaigns of 1796 and 1800 had routinely featured printed attacks on and fervid rumors about the "atheistic" Jefferson, evidence of which was alleged to be found in his work on behalf of religious freedom and, especially, the *Notes on the State of Virginia.*

For those seeking further such proof, the inaugural address might well serve the purpose: certainly by contrast it contains noticeably fewer references to the divinity than the productions of either Washington or Adams. Still, the text invokes this "overruling Providence" to strategic effect, and it would be difficult in any case to miss the overall message. The American people were blessed as no one else, and in their dispensation were assured of being made a "happy and prosperous people." To the extent that this dispensation was of a piece—that it was the divine expression of a plan authorized by nature and government as well—then those who rejected one per force rejected all. In short, Jefferson was beating the Federalists at their own game, for who could deny God's blessing thus construed?

Conclusion

Thomas Jefferson a party politician? The first inaugural an act of calculated partisanship? The very idea, it must be admitted, would have been met by the president with the strongest objections. Had he not spent the better part of the last decade—the nation's first—battling precisely those factional forces that threatened to pull down the pillars of republican government? From the very beginning, indeed, Jefferson had given pointed expression to his view of party, and he believed himself never to have wavered from his principled stance against such affiliations. Writing from Paris in March of 1789, Jefferson declared to Francis Hopkinson that he had "never submitted the whole system of my opinion to the creed of any party of men whatever in religion, in philosophy, in politics, or anything else where I was capable of thinking for myself." That kind of addiction, he insisted, "is the last degradation of a free and moral agent." For all Jefferson's protestations, however, we know that in fact he played a decisive role not only in the formation of the early Republican Party, but in doing so helped create the first organized and sustained opposition to administration policy. We are thus confronted with a paradox frequently noted by historians, the image of Jefferson-the-statesman who, in repudiating party politics, can be seen acting in the most partisan ways to effect his ideological convictions. If the first inaugural address is to be understood as arising from such contexts, we need to come to terms with this anomaly.[40]

Jefferson's anti-party partisanship may be viewed as evidence of hypocrisy, of self-delusion or failure to remain consistent in principle when expedience called. And, indeed, his enemies were prepared to convict him on all three counts. At the same time, we can see in his stance against party a set of values that had been circulating in colonial America for many years and which by the 1790s had assumed the currency of common coin. These values, it must be stressed, were known to be definitively republican, encompassing, that is, not the local or factional dogmas of a particular group, but of all Americans. They were in this sense constitutive of collective self-identity; what one thought about the role of parties in republican government said a great deal about one's claim to grasp fully the genius of the American experiment. When Jefferson spoke against the destructive forces of party, he understood himself not to be acting from partisan motives but from a venerable strain of opposition that ran back to the early years of the eighteenth century. Such views as that tradition provided, Lance Banning reminds us, "were not essentially new, but a revision of the English opposition ideology that was at the roots of American revolutionary thought. They were, in fact, so thoroughly familiar to the literate proportion of the people that, without a fully systematic explication, they were comprehended and asserted in every corner of the land."[41]

Jefferson's first inaugural address may rightfully be read as effecting the work of party ideology—this, not in spite of its high-minded idealism but on the very basis of that idealism. Put another way, it speaks to a particular set of Republican values even as it invokes a powerful tradition of anti-party thought. From Jefferson's perspective and those of his supporters, at least, there was nothing at all hypocritical, inconsistent, or deluded about such an appeal: he was merely announcing the triumph of values held by all except a small faction of crypto-monarchists who had surreptitiously seized control of the government and temporarily blinded the people to their designs. We may thus grant Jefferson's sincere conviction that he was not acting in a partisan manner even as we recognize his speech to be an ingenious political performance.

CHAPTER 2

"The Strongest Government on Earth"

The First Inaugural Address as Political Theory

America was founded, like no other republic, upon ideas. The revolution that ushered it into existence was promoted, sustained, and justified through appeals to commonly held values; the Constitution had enshrined a government of laws, not men; and the new nation was to seek its way through the turmoil of early youth by debating and deciding on which principles should point the way to a yet more perfect union. In no sense can these ideas be abstracted from the material conditions that summoned them in the first place, nor can they be said to cohere neatly into a body of theoretical statements. Revolutions and their aftermath, as we have seen in the foregoing chapter, are never so tidy as that. But America, as Hannah Arendt reminded us, survived its own birth, against odds it set for and against itself, and that fact is owing in part to the fidelity of its people to a set of collective principles. To an extent remarkable in any age, this investment in the power of ideas was the handiwork of a very few individuals. Among them, a select and small number witnessed up close the process of nation-building unfold from resistance through rebellion to settlement. They were the exceptionally gifted—the "founding brothers," in Ellis's words—who took revolutionary truths as their sacred trust, gave them voice, coherence, and effect. Among these leaders none were more eloquent, more persistent and visionary, than Thomas Jefferson.[1]

To ask after the political theory of Jefferson, to discover how such a theory was made evident and given persuasive force in the first inaugural address, would thus seem straight forward enough. Certainly the texts are there before us to be read and pondered: the *Summary View,* the Declaration, the constitutional drafts and other state papers, the Kentucky Resolutions, the voluminous correspondence—riches aplenty for anyone in search of Jefferson's political "philosophy." As is so often the case with the Sage of Monticello, however, the matter turns out to be rather more complicated than we might at first expect. In this chapter, we examine the first inaugural address as a theoretical text, as a set of statements funded by and giving added force to Jefferson's most deeply held convictions about the foundations of republican government. To arrive at such an account, however, we are first obliged to confront several preliminary and sometimes vexatious questions bearing on the sources, character, and implications of Jefferson's political thought. Having addressed, if not resolved, such questions, we turn then to consider the inaugural address as a kind of public and political treatise on those ideas thought essential to the future of the great experiment. Here we shall find Jefferson laboring to hold in productive tension two sets of republican principles as they related to *virtue and liberty* and to *national growth and foreign relations.* The theoretical achievement of the address, I suggest, resides in Jefferson's ability not to resolve these tensions but to align them in such a way as to serve best the ends of republican government.

But first things first: What kind of a theorist was Thomas Jefferson? One route to an answer is to acknowledge up front that, whatever kind of theorist he was, Jefferson's political thought was the expression of an insatiably curious mind. Natural history, science, prosody, architecture, music and fine arts, cuisine, languages, comparative government, law, religion: these and more occupied his public and private pursuits throughout his long life. Such ecumenical interests necessarily took Jefferson in a variety of different directions, and if he could not claim expertise in any one, he nonetheless may be viewed as an exemplar of the Enlightenment intellectual. They also help us discern in his political thought certain characteristics relevant to our reading of the inaugural address. Above all, we find in Jefferson's mental habits a distinctive stance toward the world, a way of engaging issues, ideas, and events that underwent little change as the years unfolded. Merrill Peterson perfectly captures the pitch: Jefferson's understanding, he writes, "spanned an immense field but spanned much of it at second- or third-hand, which gave a certain airiness to his traffic with reality. He gained a vantage point above or outside of things as-they-are—the hard crust of history—from which to perceive, as through the eye of reason, things as-they-might-be."[2]

Whether this mode of apprehending the world was a "vantage point" or not depends now, as then, on how one is inclined to judge the "Jeffersonian legacy." As an iconic figure in American history, Jefferson is usually granted the benefit of his reputation as a founder, and we are more apt now to embrace his idealism than to criticize its evident shortcomings. This has not always been the case, nor is Jefferson's stature as a political thinker altogether secure today. In his own time, he was routinely chastised by his opponents as a visionary and weightless thinker, dangerously naive as to the realities of popular forces and given to the most heretical opinions as to the province of God, government, and democratic government. Jefferson stood out, according to John Marshall, among "democrats" as a particularly egregious example of "speculative theorists," nothing more, in the words of Thomas Pickering, than a "moonshine philosopher of Monticello." Jefferson's mind, wrote John Adams, was "soured, yet seeking for popularity, and eaten to a honeycomb with ambition, yet weak, confused, uninformed, and ignorant." To his friends, on the other hand, this "moonshine philosopher" was in truth "more deeply versed in human nature and human learning than almost the whole tribe of his opponents and revilers," nothing less, in John Beckley's view, than "this philosopher of the world."[3]

The contemporary state of Jefferson's reputation as a political theorist remains unsettled. Though less obviously partisan, it continues to prompt competing assessments from his most insightful students; indeed, there appears to be no end in sight to debates over Jefferson's place in the pantheon of American heroes. Some of this has to do with recent contests associated with Jefferson's relationship to slavery and, more specifically, the Sally Hemings controversy. More generally, scholarly views of Jeffersonian political thought may be observed from one of three positions. In one line of thought, Jefferson is seen positively as providing a systematic and explicable body of precepts from which we have yet much to learn. Thus Garrett Ward Sheldon insists that Jefferson "was able to accommodate seemingly disparate elements within an original and remarkably coherent worldview to provide a more sophisticated understanding of the ideological foundations of our republic." In different ways to different ends, both Morton White and Joyce Appleby recognize in Jeffersonian thought a rich and productive basis for explaining the philosophy of the American Revolution and the origins of liberalism respectively. And Michael Zuckert, most recently, advances his powerful account of natural rights thinking in American culture on the view that "Jefferson's thought has more coherence and connectedness, more reasoning and analysis, than he is often credited with," especially as they address "human freedom and equality, and their important accompaniment, natural (or human) rights." To the question, then, of Jefferson's stature, these and other scholars firmly defend their subject as a systematic thinker, of considerable depth and influence in American political thought.[4]

Even among those for the most part appreciative of that influence, however, there remains a suspicion that Jefferson's cast of mind—that "airiness" to which Peterson alludes—was something less than the stuff of stringent theoretical reasoning. Jefferson held his opinions strongly, defended them with warmth, and pressed them assiduously on the American political landscape; but that is not the same thing as offering up a genuinely coherent theory of politics. He had, rather, a "habit of adapting strongly felt moral and political positions without fully or rigorously thinking out the implications," writes J. R. Pole; neither could Jefferson profess "so much a self consistent system of thought as an outlook on life, a composition of imperfectly reconciled sentiments and opinions, and sometimes impasses."[5]

Robert Booth Fowler, a particularly astute reader of Jefferson's prose craft, appears to agree that he was no great philosopher, but shades our picture of Jefferson-the-theorist by stressing different standards for evaluation. "Jefferson was not especially philosophical or creative or unique as a political thinker," Fowler writes, "and he did not claim to be—but he was a master of uncommonly effective expression of common American ideas, ideas that have changed the world." Such ambivalence as to Jefferson's capacity for reflection on the nature of politics is especially evident in the acclaimed work of Joseph Ellis, who has forcefully described the Sage's mind in all its peculiar and fascinating texture. The essence of that mind, Ellis argues, was a capacity for rendering the world into two competing narratives and inscribing himself indelibly into the preferred story. Again, however, that skill may be taken as talent of a kind—but not of the kind up to the task of articulating complex political phenomena. "Jefferson's mind consistently saw the world in terms of clashing dichotomies: Whigs versus Tories; moderns versus ancients; America versus Europe; rural conditions versus urban; whites versus blacks. The list could go on," Ellis concludes, "but it always came down to the forces of light against the forces of darkness, with no room for anything in between."[6]

Jefferson the systematic and comprehensive political theorist; Jefferson the eclectic promoter of popular truths and simplified verities: in either case, we have in these two perspectives little to work with as a basis for reading the first inaugural address. On the one hand, the text plainly contains a coherent statement of the speaker's most cherished convictions, and these he expresses, in his own words, as "the creed of our political faith, the text of our civic instruction, the touchstone by which to try the services of those we trust." But as a brief speech prompted by the ritual of office-taking, the inaugural address can scarcely be made to bear the weight of a comprehensive political philosophy, with all the detailed reasoning from axioms and warrants such a work requires. As a political and partisan performance, on the other hand, the speech clearly bears the hallmarks of its time and place: Jefferson had real work to do, and he meant to effect his political agenda in ways directly responsive to the circumstances of its delivery. Nevertheless, we know that it was something more than a passing effort at polemic, that it offered to his audience and to us a clearly articulated statement of Jefferson's principles in a way that was meant to endear those principles for generations yet unborn.

Thus a third approach to framing the address recommends itself to our attention. In this sense, Jefferson is best conceived as both a theorist and a practitioner of the art of politics, speaking at once to the moment and to the ages. Given the exigent demands of his world, Jefferson was obliged, as Daniel Boorstin put it, "to describe his cosmos, not in spacious treatises, but in discrete and extremely topical letters, speeches, pamphlets, and articles. His philosophy was left implicit, in the interstices between observations on particular projects." Between the rigorous search for first principles and the merely persuasive, Jefferson discovered a middle ground that, while not conceding much to either, still allowed him to buttress his appeals with truth and to give those truths maximum appeal. "Throughout his public career," Dumas Malone wrote, Jefferson "was a statesman as well as a thinker, and, since he may not qualify as a philosopher on technical grounds, he can be safely described as a philosophical statesman." A republican version of Edmund Burke's "philosopher-in-action," Jefferson exemplified that rare capacity to take ideas as seriously as the means required to put them into effect. He was not, Colin Bonwick acknowledges, "a systematic and professional philosopher, but a philosopher and a working politician who was obliged to practice his art in a frequently changing world."[7]

Theory into action and back again: if a pathway into Jefferson's political thought may be thus traced, we have then a clue to reading his first inaugural address. It remains to identify the content and movement of that thought in the text, specifically with respect to the virtue-liberty, domestic-foreign affairs pairings. Along the way, we are to be mindful that in no sense ought these concepts be abstracted into a "pure" realm of philosophy detached from the pragmatic purposes of the speech, and we need as well to acknowledge that the particular meaning and relative weight accorded to them remain under continual revision by Jefferson scholars.

VIRTUE AND THE COMMON GOOD

In the midst of party wrangling shortly before the presidential election of 1800, Jefferson composed an illuminating letter to William Green Munford. "I am among those who think well of human character generally," he confided to the young college student. "I consider man as formed for society, and endowed by nature with those dispositions which fit him for society." The sentiment is classically Jeffersonian, gesturing at once to the optimism that sustained him through the highs and lows of political life, and underscoring the basis on which that optimism rested. Nature, that all-encompassing first and final authority, had determined that humans were most human as they arranged themselves in the company of others. Drawing broadly from the Scottish tradition of moral sense philosophy, Jefferson grounded his views on the principle that we are—all of us—equipped with an innate moral sense, a natural propensity, in the words of Francis Hutchenson, to "approve every kind affection either in ourselves or others and all publicly useful actions which we imagine flow from such affections, without our having a view to our private happiness in our approbation of these actions." In other words, humans possess a moral core, an inherent capacity to perceive right and wrong and to act on that basis with and on behalf of other human beings. This capacity we call virtue, "the natural principle of attraction in man towards man."[8]

Social and political creature that he was, Jefferson had little time to systematically explore the subtle twists and turns marking this tradition, nor did he write a sustained account of his reflections on the matter. On another level, however, he did express clearly the rudiments of his conviction that humans were by nature moral and that morality was best suited to the ends of social welfare. In a letter to Peter Carr, Jefferson insisted that "man was destined for society. His morality therefore was to be formed to this object. He was endowed with a sense of right and wrong merely relative to this. This sense is as much a part of his nature as the sense of hearing, seeing; it is the true foundation of morality . . . as much a part of man as his leg or arm." Almost two decades later, Jefferson returned to the question of the moral sense and its natural tendencies. Writing to Thomas Law in 1814, the retired president explained that "nature hath implanted in our breasts a love of others, a sense of duty to them, a moral instinct, in short, which prompts us irresistibly to feel and to succor their distresses. . . . The Creator would indeed have been a bungling artist," Jefferson reasoned, "had he intended man for a social animal, without planting in him social dispositions."[9]

Jefferson's confidence in the moral sense goes a long way toward accounting for what we might call the politics of optimism. Indeed, it would be difficult to otherwise explain the resolute idealism that marks so many of his writings and the first inaugural address in particular. That it would find a receptive audience, moreover, is confirmed by the fact that he was, characteristically, giving voice to the common sense of his time; as Gordon Wood writes, "[T]here was hardly an educated person in all of eighteenth-century America who did not at one time or another try to describe people's moral sense and the natural forces of love and benevolence holding society together. Jefferson's emphasis on the moral sense was scarcely peculiar to him." But his musings on it were desultory at best. Because we require a clear sense of what is assumed and implied by those musings, it will be useful to rely on the painstaking work of Jean Yarbrough to summarize for us the constituent features of virtue thus understood: (1) it is universal, "natural to all human beings everywhere"; (2) it is distinct from and not dependent on reason, arising, rather, "out of certain moral sentiments that are inherent in our nature as social beings"; (3) although intrinsic and universal, it may be developed, indeed requires "continual exercise and encouragement to develop into the established habits and dispositions that form our character"; and (4) it is most fully realized as it is devoted to the common good; thus "the virtues that emerge as the most praiseworthy are those that preserve and perfect us as social creatures."[10]

Jefferson's interest in the naturalistic bases of virtue was no diversion from the more practical concerns before him. To the contrary, it underwrote a great deal of what he thought, said, and wrote, and we enrich our reading of the first inaugural address measurably by taking it into systematic account. In doing so, however, we confront a second theme in the speech—liberty—that complicates the effort in important ways. Broadly considered, the concept of virtue has been treated in certain scholarly discussions as pulling away from or competing with liberty as the central organizing principle of eighteenth-century political thought. In this view, virtue is located within a civic republican paradigm shaping politics during the period. It is accordingly associated with such classical values as simplicity, frugality, agrarianism, and commitment to the commonweal. By distinction, "the glorious publick Virtue so predominant in our rising Country," as Benjamin Franklin put it, was meant above all to stress the necessity of subordinating private happiness to the public good. Because a republican form of government rested first and ultimately upon the people themselves, the people were expected to contribute to the polity in ways beneficial to that government. "In a republic," explains Wood, "each man must somehow be persuaded to submerge his personal wants into the greater good of the whole. This willingness of the individual to sacrifice his private interests for the good of the community—such patriotism or love of country—the eighteenth century termed 'public virtue.' A republic was such a delicate polity precisely because it demanded an extraordinary moral character in the people." Conversely, as Lance Banning notes, "a nation in which individuals or groups are bent on private gain and personal pursuits will sink into anarchic chaos or fail to guard its freedom from tyrannical design." Virtue was thus at the heart of the republican enterprise, a communitarian principle without which the republic was surely doomed.[11]

Such a conception of virtue stands, if not in contrast to, then in uneasy tension with a second dominant theme in eighteenth-century political thought. Liberty by distinction celebrated a constellation of values frequently related to what we now call the liberal tradition in American culture—that is, a set of commitments emphasizing the priority of rights, individualism, the pursuit of private happiness, economic mobility and progress, commerce, and market capitalism. Exponents of the liberal paradigm stress that the early republic had in effect turned its back on classical understandings of civic virtue; as forward-looking, acquisitive, and aggressively independent, its citizens demanded protection from the intrusions of government and politics;

access to expanding markets and the prosperity those markets made possible; and the right to pursue their private happiness in any way they wished without harm to others. "Deliverance from the strictures of classical republicanism," Joyce Appleby contends,

> came from the ideology of liberalism, from a belief in a natural harmony of benignly striving individuals saved from chaos by the stability worked into nature's own design. First expressed in very local clashes over economic rights in the middle decades of the eighteenth century, this naturalistic recasting of human experience appeared as the universal law of self-interest among radical agitators of the 1760s and acquired final validation as part of the plan of nature and of nature's God in Thomas Jefferson's apotheosis to individual liberty.[12]

At the risk of reducing complex ideological dynamics to a set of binary oppositions, we can see at least this much: that from the perspective of the civic republican paradigm, Jefferson exemplified a tradition of thought that enshrined virtue as a quintessentially public value. Nature had installed in humans deeply social instincts, the greatest expression of which was to act for the common good. By extension, as Garrett Sheldon argues, "politics for Jefferson could not be limited to purely liberal strictures of protecting private rights and individual interests. Rather, the moral sense, which included knowledge and choice of the good, sympathy for others' sufferings, and concern for the well-being of society generally, constituted a public sense of virtue, requiring both education and practice in political life." From the liberal perspective, alternately, Jefferson can be seen as the champion of individual rights, limited government, and economic expansion. If anything, Appleby counters, Jefferson "reversed the priorities implicit in the classical tradition. The private came first. Instead of regarding the public arena as the locus of human fulfillment where men rose above their self-interest to serve the common good, Jefferson wanted government to offer protection to the personal realm where men might freely exercise their faculties."[13]

The debate over Jefferson's role in either ideological formation continues to be productive, and it is rather more complex than is represented here. For our purposes, however, it serves not only to highlight two major themes in the first inaugural, but suggests a way by which those themes might be interpreted. Recalling Joseph Ellis's reference to the "natural harmonies he heard inside his own head," we can plausibly ask whether Jefferson himself felt torn by the competing pulls of virtue and liberty. At least to his own satisfaction, I suggest, he did not. The inaugural address rather gives evidence that he saw these two commitments as representing either side of the republican coin, indeed that the nation would survive and prosper precisely to the extent that both civic virtue and liberal republicanism were retained as powerful rationales for political action. In the following we trace the contours of both these rationales as they appear in the speech, seeking not to resolve one into the other, nor to give one priority; the aim, rather, is to see how Jefferson gives each its considered and rightful due.

Private happiness and the public good were not for Jefferson aligned against each other but mutually constitutive. To act on behalf of the latter implied no concession to the former: it was to see in one the means to the other. To be a citizen in this sense was to occupy the highest station of one's humanity, for that person was truly a patriot who acted in concert and according to law as an agent of republican government. This will-to-community was in fact virtue itself, defined by Montesquieu "as the love of the laws and of our country. As such love requires a constant preference of public to private interests, it is the source," wrote the French philosopher, "of all private virtues; for they are nothing more than this very preference itself." The second paragraph of Jefferson's inaugural address provides convincing evidence that such a conception of virtue was very much at the heart of his republican vision. Taken as a whole, the paragraph may be said to represent one side of a more general calculus, balancing in steady equipoise a scale weighted on the other side by what we have called Jefferson's liberal principles. Virtue is here summoned and put on display with reference to at least four key principles: the "voice of the nation"; "common efforts for the common good"; "harmony and affection"; and the role of "private concern" in facing "invasions of the public order."[14]

The intense partisanship of the 1790s, as we have seen, had startled disputants on both sides. Federalists and Republicans alike had anguished over the state of the union, indeed at times wondered if the sinews of the young government were strong enough to withstand the stresses placed on them by the organized self-interest that was party warfare. In what sense, really, did it even make sense to speak of the "union" when contending parties sought to take as their own that which belonged to all? The "revolution of 1800," by contrast, seemed to Jefferson and his supporters a sign not only that concord was to be restored, but nationhood itself. The contest had been decided, Jefferson declares in the speech, "by the voice of the nation." That voice, "announced according to the rules of the Constitution," was to be heard as more than the shout from the polls: it was proof positive that the people had put divisive self-interest behind them, had exerted themselves through common sense on behalf of the common good. "The mighty wave of public opinion," Jefferson later marveled, had written a new chapter in the republican story, heralding in the process "a strength of character in our nation which augurs well for the duration of our Republick."[15]

Jefferson was convinced throughout his life that humans were possessed of a moral instinct, and this he thought "the brightest gem with which the human character is studded, and the want of it as more degrading than the most hideous of the body deformities." Now, it was true that such a deformity had beset the body politic in the decade preceding his election to the presidency; indeed few were more active than the speaker in diagnosing (and, his critics argued, exacerbating) that disease. This much was perhaps to be expected now and then, for as Yarbrough reminds us, the moral sense did not guarantee that humans would always and everywhere act according to its dictates. But Jefferson's unfailing optimism prompted him to expect that, though the people had been temporarily debased, they would in time see their way toward genuine happiness. The 1790s was one such period of degeneration, yet all Jefferson and his countrymen had to do was look out at the scene before them to realize that the health of the republic had been fully restored.[16]

And none too soon, for the stakes could not have been higher. Without this reassertion of public virtue, "without some portion of this generous principle, anarchy and confusion would immediately ensue, the jarring interests of individuals, regarding themselves only, and indifferent to the welfare of others, would still further heighten the distressing scene, and with the assistance of the selfish passions, it would end in the ruin and subversion of the state." But the voice of the nation had spoken, its virtue and Jefferson's confidence vindicated, and he could now announce without hesitation that "all will, of course, arrange themselves under the will of the law, and unite in common efforts for the common good." In the context of Jefferson's thought generally and the speech specifically, the phrase "of course" takes on a significance equal to the more conspicuous "common efforts for the common good." In its eighteenth-century sense, it suggests the force of natural law, as we may recall from the resonant opening lines of the Declaration of Independence. Here, Jefferson stresses that conditions have been recalled to their rightful order, where that the laws of nature may be effected to their ends in the common good.[17]

Classically understood, virtue assumed that humans found their greatest happiness in public life—in deliberating about issues of collective concern, establishing laws, ensuring the well being of the polity of which all were a part. That conception is Aristotle's, and Jefferson clearly shared in certain of its precepts. But it is important to note as well that he viewed politics as the product, or the effect, of something which comes before. Individuals were by nature social and thus organized themselves in relation to one another; politics was but the extension in certain terms of this organization, and therefore must bear its impressions. By implication, politics could not change human nature, but human nature can and will change politics. This is why for Jefferson that politics is best which best accommodates individual and social expressions of natural law. When he famously declared in the *Notes on the State of Virginia* that "those who labour in the earth are the chosen people of God, if ever he had a chosen people, whose breasts he has made his peculiar deposit for substantial and genuine virtue," Jefferson was in effect arguing that any government claiming legitimacy must adapt itself to the virtues of the people in whom it finds the source of authority in the first place. In short, a political arrangement is only as a good as the society it mirrors. And this is why Jefferson seeks so earnestly in the inaugural address to mend the rent fabric of social life: "Let us, then, fellow-citizens, unite with one heart and one mind. Let us restore to social intercourse that harmony and affection without which liberty and even life itself are but dreary things." Given what we know of Jefferson's belief in the moral sense and the ways this sense finds its natural expression in social and political life, we can read in these lines not so much the musings of a visionary utopian as an idealized conception of polity made plausible again by the laws of nature and of nature's God.[18]

Jefferson's triumph in the election of 1800 proved to his own satisfaction, at least, that those laws were very much in play. He did not have to argue the point at length: had not the nation spoken with one voice? Had not the people united for the common good? Had not civility been restored? These, it seemed, were plain facts, placed just where Jefferson liked them: before the eyes. To be sure, there remained the doubters— two of them were by his side—but the indisputable thing, the most dramatic fact of all, was that the people had swept Jefferson into power and with him the future of republicanism itself. Here was evidence if any was needed that the people were in truth virtuous, that they were capable of placing love of country above self-serving ambition. Years later Jefferson could account for this fact with recourse again to the theory of innate moral sense, believing, he wrote, "our relations with others as constituting the boundaries of morality . . . Self-love, therefore, is no part of morality. Indeed it is exactly its counterpart." This self-love, explained Jefferson, "is the sole antagonist of virtue, leading us constantly by our propensities to self-gratification in violation of our moral duties to others."[19]

In its republican context, this moral duty to others takes on exceptional weight, for it was nothing less than the foundation on which such government rests. Again, republicanism could be only as strong as the people who authorized it, and that strength was its virtue. Everything depended on it. The key marker of this virtue, its most precise measure, was the capacity of the private individual to so identify with the public good that a threat to one was a threat necessarily to the other. In the words of the revolutionary John Hurt, this sense of the public good made of it a "common bank in which every individual has his respective share; and consequently whatever damage that it sustains the individual unavoidably partake of that calamity." Now, the second revolution, the republican revolution of 1800, had demonstrated just this kind of investment in the bank of the public good; the result, Jefferson said, was "the strongest Government on earth," the only one, he insisted, "where everyman, at the call of the law, would fly to the standard of the law, and would meet invasions of the public order as his own personal concern." Here in its essence is the best that the civic republican and moral sense philosophies had to offer Jefferson in his moment of triumph. Together, through the wisdom of history and insights of reason, they fused a conception of polity that was something more than politics, and they gave to nature an object that was something more than mere survival. That something was "virtue," at once the origin and horizon of human community.[20]

LIBERTY AND THE SUM OF GOOD GOVERNMENT

Jefferson is rightly accorded pride of place among the founders as the apostle of liberty. From his defiant declaration in the *Summary View* that "the God who gave us life gave us liberty at the same time" to his final assurance shortly before death that "all eyes are opened, or opening, to the rights of man," Jefferson never ceased thinking about this quintessentially American value. None wrote more poignantly of its blessings, and none, consequently, drew more attention to the paradox of a life so dedicated as an owner of human chattel. In addition to that haunting reality, our task in arriving at a comprehensive and coherent account of Jefferson's thoughts on liberty is made more complicated by several facts. He composed no systematic treatment of the subject; as is so often the case with Jefferson, we must rather glean from among his diffuse writings and hope only to approximate a true representation. His views of the nature and province of liberty, moreover, may well have changed in the course of his long and eventful life. And, finally, Jefferson's conception of liberty continues to undergo scholarly reassessment and debate. Although we cannot trace in any detail the course of his thinking or the many and various attempts to interpret it, we do need to arrive at a general sense of what he meant by the concept and how that meaning may be applied to our reading of the inaugural address. The key to this reading, again, is to recognize that Jefferson saw no inherent or inevitable contest between liberty and virtue; it was rather the very genius of republican government to hold in productive tension the will to individual happiness and the imperatives of civic responsibility.[21]

We may start by asking what liberty meant to the eighteenth-century citizen. As disparate and vague as the term might seem, it was in truth used so frequently in so many local contexts with such similar intentions that a fairly ready answer can be had. For Moses Mather, liberty referred simply to "the power of a Civil Society or State to govern itself by its own discretions; or by the laws of its own discretion." At issue here was the source, place, and function of sovereign power, understood by republicans everywhere to be found in the people themselves and their duly established institutions of government. Thus for Benjamin Church, "the liberty of the people is exactly proportioned to the share the body of the people have in the legislature; and the check placed in the constitution, on the executive power." The particular weighting of such power, its reach and balance among component parts of the government, was and would remain very much a matter of adjustment. But "that the will of the people is the supreme law in all republican governments," most Americans agreed; and no surprise, for here "the human mind, free as the air, may exert all its powers toward the various objects laid before it, and expand its faculties to an extent hitherto unknown." In founding their republic on such principles, Enos Hitchcock boasted, Americans had created a government "most congenial to the rights of man, and the enjoyment of equal liberty—that liberty, which to independence unites security—which to the most ample elective powers, unites strength and energy in government."[22]

We have seen that with respect to virtue, eighteenth-century writers imposed no hard and fast contrasts between private and public expressions of that quality. They stood as interdependent variations on the same theme. Similarly, we need to understand liberty as referring not to the simple activation of individual will, nor exclusively as the provision of a given political order. Liberty was understood rather as "the combining of each man's individual liberty into a collective governmental authority, the institutionalization of the people's personal liberty, making public or political liberty equivalent to democracy or government by the people themselves." In this sense, as Lance Banning explains, liberty could signify "both private liberties such as property rights and religious freedom and public liberty as embodied in the practice of popular self-government." Finally, liberty thus conceived emphatically did not entail unchecked expression of popular power. Republican spokesmen were adamant on this point, for, in the words of Peter Thacher, "without government, indeed without law and order, there is no liberty, no security, no peace or prosperity. Men ought to guard their right," the clergyman intoned, "they ought to resist arbitrary power of every kind; they ought to establish a free government; but no people can be safe, no nation can be happy where 'every man does what is right in his own eyes,' and the people are driven about by the whirlwind of their passions." In sum, liberty was meant to designate power as held by the people, at once a personal and public blessing, restrained by law and accruing to the advantage of all citizens equally.[23]

Against this general backdrop Jefferson's conception of liberty may be illuminated—at least enough to shed light on the first inaugural address. It must be acknowledged up front that his views are not entirely assimilable to a uniform definition of liberty in the eighteenth century, in part because there can be no such definition, in part because he may be said to have held them more radically than many of his compatriots. Jefferson habitually posed liberty against that shibboleth of the era, power, and he was more inclined than most to countenance what others feared as the extreme and unfortunate expressions of the liberal temperament ("a little rebellion now and then is a good

thing"). In any case, Jefferson's thinking on liberty may be characterized as bearing recurrently on a finite set of concerns; in identifying
them, we can approach the inaugural address with some sense of confidence that what we see therein is representative of his thought generally. At a minimum, this set would include liberty of conscience, under
which we can arrange such "private rights" as freedom of religion, press,
and protest. On behalf of these liberties Jefferson memorably "swore,
upon the alter of god, eternal hostility against every form of tyranny
over the mind of man." Such freedoms we might cautiously refer to as
private liberties. A second set, closely related, includes injunctions
against the power of government, either as it is asserted against private
ambition or the rights of states to exercise sovereign authority. Here is
the Jefferson insistent that the people were "the only censors of their
government," that "free government is founded in jealousy; and not in
confidence."[24]

These sets are in reality distinguishable for synoptic purposes only,
but they provide us a useful means of discerning in the inaugural address two key themes. More specifically, we will find that the text stages
a classically Jeffersonian drama, where his commitment to public liberty is accompanied by images of restraint on governmental power, and
his commitment to private liberty by images of release, of the unfettered individual reaching his potential under conditions of optimal
freedom. This play of restraint and release will serve to group Jefferson's
statements on liberty in the text, and serve as well to describe the manner in which his principles are given effective expression. We will see,
finally, that in so communicating his views, Jefferson artfully sustains a
preferred relationship between liberty and virtue, the synthesis of which
tightens the fabric of his text and blends its distinctive colors into a
clear pattern of meaning.

In her landmark lectures collected as *Capitalism and the New Social
Order,* the distinguished historian Joyce Appleby organizes eighteenth-
century views of liberty into three predominant categories. These include the liberty to participate in public affairs, which she associates
with the classical republican tradition; the liberty of secure possession,
a "negative" construction guaranteed by charter; and the liberty to

exercise one's rights as an autonomous individual in pursuit of natural and God-given rights. In the last of these liberties we locate a preoccupation of Jefferson's, evident not only in the inaugural speech but
in virtually all of his major writings and in a good deal of his personal
correspondence. It is the liberty enshrined as a self-evident truth in the
Declaration, the liberty of which Jefferson wrote in the Bill for Establishing Religious Freedom ("that Almighty God hath created the mind
free, and manifested his supreme will that free it shall remain by making it altogether free of restraint"). It is the liberty in defense of which
he summoned his countrymen in a letter to William Green Munford:
"To preserve the freedom of the human mind then, and freedom of
the press," Jefferson then declared, "every spirit should be ready to de-
vote to martyrdom; for as long as we may think as we will, and speak
as we think, the condition of man will proceed in improvement."
Jefferson's unwavering confidence that mankind will in fact so proceed
was the result of his conviction that humans were encouraged by nature to actualize their God-given talents. Republican government, because it was that political arrangement best suited to such ends, was
thus understood as a kind of artful construction for the play of nature's
design."[25]

The first inaugural address does not just invoke this liberty—it turns
a commonplace in eighteenth-century thought into a principle on
which the future of republican government depends. Recalling his reference to America as "a chosen country," we are alerted to the double-
sense that phrase contains, a country, that is, singled out by God and
bestowed with the blessings of nature, but chosen, too, by the people
themselves. Americans in this sense had in the very act of revolution
and state-making exercised their right of conscience to effect a new
nation, a *novus ordo seclorum*. They had acted freely to secure freedom,
and in doing so laid claim to a vast canvass on which to advance their
individual and collective wills. The imagery throughout the speech is
devoted to capturing the drama of a people released—released from
the past, from tyranny, from the artificial and destructive bonds of the
old order. Nature had separated America from the havoc of Europe,
had provided "room enough for our descendants to the thousandth

and thousandth generation," and had ensured "our equal right to the use of our own faculties, to the acquisition of our own industry."

In its most elemental sense, the power of the people rested in the capacity to release and exercise those energies bestowed by providence. Government was at its best when it made way for these energies; indeed its only legitimate function was to ensure conditions for the positive and productive expression of the human spirit; hence Jefferson's renewed call for "encouragement of agriculture, and of commerce as its handmaiden; the diffusion of information and arraignment of all abuses at the bar of public reason; freedom of religion; freedom of the press, and freedom of person under the protection of the habeas corpus, and trial by juries impartially selected." These freedoms and more had of course been installed constitutionally, and though suppressed in the past few years, remained as Jefferson wished they should, as the "creed of our political faith." And the basis of that faith was unmistakably a faith in the power of the people to act wisely in freedom. "The American republic found its unity in an idea," Merrill Peterson aptly concludes, and "drew its strength from the energies of a free, enlightened, and virtuous society; and unlike great monarchies, it would remain strong only as it grew in the affections of the people."[26]

The affections of the people: here was the rub. For Jefferson and others, the question was how to sustain "political faith" in the principles of republican government in such a way as to ensure its success and that of the people themselves. The problem, even for so sanguinary a mind as Jefferson's, was that government could not even at its best be made entirely synonymous with the will of the people. As a structure of delegated authority, its power was inevitably at some remove from the sovereign source on whom that power was applied. That much was the price paid for a government at once federated and national. Power, as Jefferson and virtually all eighteenth-century observers agreed, tended to work against the tides of virtue; it aggregated to itself ever greater resources for working its will against popular liberties. In this Jefferson drew from a rich body of seventeenth- and eighteenth-century opposition thought associated with the English Whig tradition of opposition writing. Power was known in this tradition, Bernard Bailyn explains, for "its essential characteristic of aggressiveness; its endlessly propulsive tendency to expand itself beyond legitimate boundaries," the more fearsome because "its natural prey, its necessary victim, was liberty, or law, or right."[27]

Now, the framers of the Constitution had in principle resolved this ancient antagonism between power and liberty by locating sovereignty in the people; that was at once its genius and the very definition of republican government. It is fair to say, however, that Jefferson never fully reconciled himself to this solution—not because he lacked faith in the people, but because he so feared that "essential characteristic of aggressiveness" to which Bailyn alludes. To a degree this anxiety may be attributed to the distinctive cast of Jefferson's mind, where James Read identifies an unshakable "suspicion of political power: his belief in an eternal struggle between the power of government and liberty of citizens—an unequal struggle in which all the advantages lie on the side of power." In this context, Read notes, the "task for the statesman is not to create or expand power—power can always take care of itself—but to fortify liberty to make the contest more equal." But the sentiment was not Jefferson's alone, and in proclaiming the revolution of 1800 he was confronted again with the paradox of popularly elected government: that the people, in seeking to secure their liberties, must delegate their powers to a distant few. Was not the very process a recipe for diminishing those liberties on which the republican experiment was constructed?[28]

Jefferson's answer to that question is complex, but in the inaugural address we see it expressed with striking efficiency. The primal location of power as sovereign in the people, we have seen, gave to liberty its animus and direction. It enabled citizens to act as free and autonomous agents of their own future. Hence the image of release that colors so much of the text. The requisite delegation of that power—or at least some of it—to elected authorities conversely asserts a principle of restraint. To gain a bit of perspective on that principle, we might remind ourselves of Jefferson's affinity for Lockean thought on these matters. "Men join and unite into a community," Locke wrote, "for their comfortable, safe and peaceful living one amongst another, in a secure Enjoyment of their Properties, and a greater Security against any that are not of it." When government fails to secure the ends of community thus joined or otherwise acts "contrary to the common interest of the People," then the people "are at Liberty to provide for themselves by erecting a new Legislature." With this contractual theory of government Jefferson could not agree more; it literally underwrote his most famous document, and he continued all his life to hold what was for some startlingly benign views about the virtues of revolution. But Jefferson's task on March 4 was not to call for yet another revolution—he sought rather to reinforce those commitments necessary to prevent such drastic measures. Republican government, in short, required that the people remain vigilant against the exercise of powers tenuously transferred from their hands into those of their leaders. This meant above all that government was to be restrained from intervening in the affairs of its citizens where no intervention was constitutionally warranted.[29]

There is nothing incidental in the fact that Jefferson first gives explicit reference to the principle of restraint immediately following the "chosen country" passage. As if to set in dramatic relief the two themes of individual liberty and limited government, he asks pointedly what, in view of "all these blessings," is "necessary to make us a happy and a prosperous people?" One more thing, Jefferson answers: "a wise and frugal Government, which shall restrain men from injuring one another, shall leave them otherwise free to regulate their own pursuits of industry and improvement, and shall not take from the mouth of labor the bread it has earned." And this, he concludes, "this is the sum of good government, and this is necessary to close the circle of our felicities." In different ways and in different contexts Jefferson had been saying the same thing for years: to Elbridge Gerry he had delivered a "profession of my political faith," in which he avowed his commitment to "a government rigorously frugal and simple," and to Philip Mazzei he claimed that "we are likely to preserve the liberty we have attained only by unremitting labors and perils. But we shall preserve them; and our mass of weight and wealth on the good side is so great, as to leave no danger that force will ever be attempted against us." Put another way, such vigilance was the natural expression of a virtuous people, whose liberties are secured not through the complacent transfer of power to government but through the relentless checking of that power as it is directed back toward them. The best measure of its success is the simplicity, frugality, and restraint that must characterize all republican government.[30]

The following paragraph represents the clearest distillation of Jefferson's creed on record. It is remarkable as well for its axiomatic character, as if in the very syntax, rhythm, and simplicity of its prose we see mirrored the image of government he would have his audience embrace. They are, Jefferson says, the "essential principles of our Government," and fittingly promises to "compress them within the narrowest compass they will bear, stating the general principle, but not all its limitations." They are:

1. "Equal and exact justice to all men, of whatever state or persuasion, religious or political;
2. peace, commerce, and honest friendship with all nations, entangling alliances with none;
3. the support of the State governments in all their rights, as the most competent administrations for our domestic concerns and the surest bulwarks against the antirepublican tendencies;
4. the preservation of the General Government in its whole constitutional vigor, as the sheet anchor of our peace at home and safety abroad;
5. a jealous care of the right of election by the people—a mild and safe corrective of abuses which are lopped by the sword of revolution where peaceable remedies are unprovided;
6. absolute acquiescence in the decisions of the majority, the vital principle of republics, from which is no appeal but to force, the vital principle and immediate parent of despotism;
7. a well-disciplined militia, our best reliance in peace and for the first moments of war till regulars may relieve them;
8. the supremacy of the civil over the military authority;
9. economy in the public expense, that labor may be lightly burthened;

10. the honest payment of our debts and sacred preservation of the public faith;
11. encouragement of agriculture, and of commerce as its handmaiden;
12. the diffusion of information and arraignment of all abuses at the bar of public opinion;
13. freedom of religion;
14. freedom of the press;
15. and freedom of person under the protection of habeas corpus;
16. and trials by juries impartially selected."

Taken together, this "text of our civic instruction" constitutes the propositional content of Jefferson's theory of public liberty. That they are familiar in the argot of eighteenth-century political thought is evidence that he sought not to introduce novel or provocative principles, but to articulate in as simple and forceful language as possible the touchstones of his republican age. Collectively, moreover, they may be seen as ties binding the reach of government; thus constrained, such centralized political authority as obtained in the national government was to be clearly demarcated, supervised, and controlled by a watchful and "jealous" citizenry. Reflecting on these principles, we see further that Jefferson meant to designate the institutional means by which the people's essential virtue could be given its most extensive ambit. In this way, the energies released through the republican experiment would conduce both to their own happiness and to that of the government. A "happy and prosperous people" left free by a "wise and frugal Government": here "the circle of our felicities" completed itself.

Virtue, Liberty, and the Nationhood

Jefferson returned from Paris late in 1789 to assume responsibilities as secretary of state in the new Washington administration. Still ambivalent about his prospects in that office, Jefferson comforted himself several months later with a letter to his French acquaintance Madame d'Enville. "I have but one system of ethics for men and for nations—to be grateful, to be faithful to all engagements and under all circumstances, to be open and generous, promotes in the long run even the interests of both; and I am sure it promotes their happiness." That system would be tested severely in the decade to come, but its expression here captures perfectly the relationship Jefferson thought obtained between public and private morality. The terms of this "system of ethics" ran directly from virtue to liberty to nationhood and back again, each presupposing the other in a complex structure of convictions.[31]

As we turn in this final section to explore Jefferson's concept of nationhood generally and as it is articulated in the first inaugural address, it will be important to keep this relationship in mind. To his critics then and now, Jefferson's nationalism has been judged abstract and diffuse; to his own way of thinking, however, nationhood—*republican* nationhood—rested its prospects on the concrete realities of lived experience and the demonstrated capacity of humans for self-government. Hence the movement from our discussion of virtue and liberty to nationhood may be understood less as a shift in contexts than a natural and necessary extension of Jefferson's thought.

The question occupying the remainder of this chapter concerns Jefferson's views on nationhood. If, as Jefferson claimed, a "system of ethics" underwrote his thinking about both individuals and nations, then we are midway to an answer. As a route to reading the first inaugural address, of course, we need a more specific and elaborate set of instructions, and these can be secured by pressing on the elemental features of Jefferson's nationalism, identifying main lines of argument, and detailing a framework within which we can read the text. The position from which we conduct this inquiry may be stated as follows: the first inaugural address contains a brief but coherent theory of nationhood; this theory is premised on the assumption that America is best served through a strategic balance of foreign and domestic interests; such a balance asserts both America's uniqueness and her vital role in international affairs; she is thus to be understood as at once exceptional without being isolated, involved globally without being subject to the contagion of Old World politics. This in summary form represents the second half of our answer, and to its elaboration we now turn.

The first generation of American citizens, wrote Tench Coxe in 1794, "have since exhibited to the world the new and interesting spectacle of a whole people, meeting, as it were, in this their political plain, and voluntarily imposing upon themselves the wholesome and necessary restraints of just government." Coxe was writing for foreign eyes what he took to be the state of republican government in the new nation. This much, in any case, would have come as news to Thomas Jefferson, who from his retirement at Monticello, was finding it increasingly difficult to retain his professed serenity. There was spectacle, to be sure: Hamilton's vaunting ambition, personal animosities played out in the press, partisan bickering, continued British depredations on the economy and dignity of the new republic, the Genet fiasco. But as to reports of a "whole people," together on the same "political plain," willingly disciplined by a restrained and "just government," Jefferson would have been incredulous. Indeed, he wrote Madison, he had stepped away from office precisely because that political plane appeared to be disintegrating, and he had grown tired beyond endurance of a "desperate and eternal contest against a host who are systematically undermining the public liberty and prosperity."[32]

Such lapses in the otherwise sanguine temper of Jefferson did not usually last long, and soon enough he was back in the thick of things. But in this, the decade of his discontent, the role of opposition leader forced Jefferson to come to terms with his vision of nationhood as never before. He had once declared his countryman's independence; he had labored to improve his state's constitution; he had ministered to his nation's French relations. But the Federalist government of the new republic was altogether new and unexpected, and Jefferson was now forcefully obliged not just to resist but to advance an alternative, coherent, and compelling vision for the new nation. Now in short was the seedtime of Jefferson's nationalism, and in tracing its growth we glimpse the ways in which his thought then nourished eventually the positions expressed in the first inaugural address. As with other dimensions of his thought, his nationalism was not always consistently conceived or expressed, but we can identify at least three paths that lead us directly to March of 1801: expansion, neutrality, and federal union.

AN EXPANDING EMPIRE OF LIBERTY

When in his inaugural address Jefferson invoked a "rising nation, spread over a wide and fruitful land," he in effect stipulated a first principle in his theory of nationhood. It was not his alone, of course: since its pre-national origins, the land that was to become a country had been conceived as both a terminus and a beginning; at once an asylum and a point of ever-expanding opportunities, where, as Berkeley wrote, "westward the course of empire takes its way." For Jefferson and virtually all Americans, the achievement of independence was not an end but a beginning, the first phase in an indefinite process of growth, prosperity, and progress. America was, in his memorable phrase, an "empire of liberty, an extensive and fertile country," whose boundaries, physical and ideological, seemed without limit.[33]

Jefferson's first administration, securing as it would the Louisiana territory and the services of Lewis and Clark, promised to prove in fact what he claimed in theory. His nationalism was thus a combustible mixture of expansionist energies, where the reach of republicanism was guided by political, cultural, and geographical ambitions the likes of which had never been seen. America's "domain and compulsions," explained Julian Boyd, "would be in the realm of the mind and spirit of man, freely and inexorably transcending political boundaries, incapable of being restrained, and holding imperial sway not by arms or political power but by the sheer majesty of ideas and ideals." Needless to say, such ideals contained little or nothing for those—Native Americans and the enslaved—who found themselves systematically excluded from the new dispensation. For those within it, however, Jefferson held out a view of nationhood that was in a sense beyond itself, a polity bound not by physical limits but emancipated from them. America was in this respect more than a geopolitical fact; it was an act of the moral imagination lit by the fires of republican faith. "American nationhood," as Peter Onuf has written, "was supposed to be the first great step toward the republican millennium, when self-governing peoples across the world would join in peaceful, prosperous harmonious union."[34]

The theory was no doubt idealistic, arguably naive, and certain to bear bitter fruit in the century ahead. But for Jefferson and his followers, at least, it was grounded in and made feasible by the realities before them. At its heart was a perspective born from looking by habit westward, away from Europe and toward a boundless land "advancing rapidly to destinies beyond the reach of mortal eye." Jefferson was absolutely certain that Americans had it in their power to pursue those destinies in a manner befitting a virtuous and freedom-loving people. The West above all meant land, and who better to make it flower than the American? "We have now lands enough to employ an infinite number of people in their cultivation," Jefferson wrote John Jay. "Cultivators of the earth are the most valuable citizens. They are the most vigorous, and they are tied to their country and wedded to its liberty and interests by the most lasting bonds." It is important to observe here that the "empire of liberty" was not reducible to land enough and people enough. For Jefferson, panegyrist to farmers everywhere ("Those who labor in the earth are the chosen people of God"), the imperial nation was to be secured by a people united in their shared commitment to republican principles. And for this reason, Jefferson insisted, "our confederacy must be viewed as the nest from which all America, North and South, is to be populated."[35]

"COMMERCE WITH ALL NATIONS, ALLIANCE WITH NONE"

A second and intimately related feature of Jefferson's nationalism has to do with the complex matter of his foreign policy. Clearly no justice can be done to this concern here: still, it is possible to note some of its general tenets and suggest how they shape the message of March 4. Several preliminary comments may help broaden our perspective. First, the westward turn in Jefferson's gaze was perforce a turning away from the horizons of the east. This point should be stated cautiously, for reasons that will become soon evident, but it is important to remind ourselves that the expansionist ideology previously discussed was only possible to the extent that a definite perspective had been established with respect to the European scene. Second, we need to acknowledge that Jefferson was seldom more of a moralist than when he sought to promote and defend his foreign policy. In this context, write Tucker and Hendrickson, Jefferson's "characteristic utterance was the contrast he drew between the high moral purpose that animated our own national life and action, and the low motives of power and expediency that drove others." This tendency has the consequence of eliminating shades that might otherwise color and complicate America's relationship to the Old World. Third, it is at times difficult to ascertain exactly what Jefferson really thought about the nation's stance before the world. At times he will frankly aver that "all the world is becoming commercial," and that therefore "we cannot separate ourselves from them." At others, he will plaintively wish "that there were an ocean of fire between us and the old world." Perhaps it is best simply to start with the assumption that when it came to foreign policy, Jefferson wished for a world in which none was needed but was realist enough to know that one was required.[36]

As announced in the first inaugural address, Jefferson's position on America's foreign relations was as idealistic as it was precise: "peace, commerce, and honest friendship with all nations, entangling alliances with none." This much is less a policy, of course, than a premise, and in giving it voice Jefferson was echoing a commonplace of the time. Who would dare wish otherwise? Bidding farewell to his countrymen, George Washington had unequivocally stated that the "great rule of conduct for us in regard to foreign nations is in extending our commercial relations, to have with them as little connection as possible," and John Adams inaugurated his presidency by promising "an inflexible determination to maintain peace and inviolable faith with all nations, and that system of neutrality and impartiality among the belligerent powers of Europe which has been adopted by this government." For all their insistence that she remain free from such "entangling alliances," each knew that America never was and never could be isolated from world affairs; hence the imperative to strike that optimal balance between domestic self-interest and foreign alliance on which the fortunes of the new nation rested. No one was more keenly alive to this imperative than Jefferson, who had spent the better part of his career negotiating its intricate demands. Some of the battles he won, others he lost. But one thing was self-evident: the less America had to do with Europe, the better.[37]

"The success and prosperity of Jefferson's republican empire," Peter Onuf has written, "depended on disentangling and distinguishing America from Europe, freedom-loving republicans from vicious and corrupt sovereigns and subjects." But how? Jefferson's own record suggests something of the difficulty he had in coming to terms with a satisfying answer. It is thus important to our understanding of the first inaugural address that we see in its stance toward Europe the culmination of a long and often frustrating struggle. Jefferson had once championed France's revolutionary ambitions, had seen in them a European counterpart to the American experiment in liberty. Together, he had then believed, France and America might lead the Old and New Worlds toward the "republican millennium" that seemed so close at hand. With the advent of the "terror" and the coming of the Napoleonic wars those hopes faded, and by decade's end Jefferson had clearly arrived at a different view. He knew very well that Europe could not be simply wished away; nonetheless he hoped that a principled neutrality might not only free Americans from ruinous commitments but unite them against a common enemy. "Better keep together as we are," he told John Taylor of Caroline, "hawl off from Europe as soon as we can, and from all attachments to any portion of it. And if we feel their power just sufficiently to hoop us together, it will be the happiest situation in which we can exist." Such hooping was conspicuously absent so far, but that was because no genuine neutrality had yet been exercised. Jefferson aimed to change all that. "I am for free commerce with all nations," he proclaimed to Elbridge Gerry, "political connection with none; and little or no diplomatic establishment. And I am not for linking ourselves by new treaties with the quarrels of Europe; entering that field of slaughter to preserve their balance, or joining in the confederacy of kings to war against the principle of liberty."[38]

In declaring his commitment to "free commerce with all nations," Jefferson alerts us to a second and fundamental component of his thoughts on foreign affairs. There has been a good deal of scholarship devoted to the question of just how enthusiastic Jefferson was about the role of commerce in the new nation. Was he, as Banning and others have suggested, dubious about capitalism and its effects on American virtue, or was he, as Appleby has argued, anxious to ensure his country a vital place in the newly emerging world of trade, manufacture, and finance? Not surprisingly, passages from Jefferson's writings may be lifted to support either contention, and we are left with no obvious answer to the question. At best we can say that he feared the excesses thought to mark economies devoted to commerce alone; hence his repulsion from urban, market-based centers of manufacture that threatened to undo the agrarian values definitive of American society. On the other hand, we cannot doubt that Jefferson thought commerce in some version to be essential to the growth and security of the nation. The real question was therefore not whether America would be integrated into the international economic scene, but how and on whose terms. And that question lead him immediately to discern that domestic and foreign relations bore directly on each other. Jefferson's thinking on this issue was, notes Walter Lafeber, "a classic example of how the American domestic political economy is inseparable from its foreign policies, and how those policies in turn make demands on domestic political and economic institutions and ideology."[39]

This much was certain: the health of the nation at home was to a significant degree a function of its health abroad. Such health in turn was assured to the extent that two conditions were met: peace and free trade. Put another way, Jefferson realized as few others did before him that commerce could be utilized as a substitute for and antidote to military force. We find, for example, that when speaking of neutrality he frequently includes in the same passage prescriptions for peace and commerce. It was not simply that Jefferson was a peaceful man; he was that, although he could entertain special circumstances requiring force of arms. It was rather that commerce was in the main more effective as a tool for exercising the national will. "War is not the best engine for us to resort to," Jefferson claimed in a letter to Thomas Pinckney, if only because "nature has given us one in our commerce, which, if properly managed, will be a better instrument for obliging the interested nations of Europe to treat us with justice." Jefferson was to confront the limits of this doctrine during his last administration, but for now commerce seemed the ideal means to have it both ways, to ensure American prosperity on American terms. The world was becoming commercial, as he told Washington, and if it were "practicable to keep our new empire separated from them we might indulge ourselves in speculating whether commerce contributes to the happiness of mankind." The reality, however, was that such a stance was not practicable, that "we cannot separate ourselves from them." In the twin commitments to peace and free trade, Jefferson had found a way to make that reality not only tolerable but a national blessing.[40]

THE BONDS OF UNION

The historian Colin Bonwick reminds us of a simple but remarkable fact. America was originally composed from but thirteen of twenty colonies poised on the edge of a distant and troubled empire. There was nothing natural or inevitable about the process through which these were formed into united states, no obvious ties that bound them, in all their differences, together into one whole. "The development of the American Union after independence," Bonwick observes, "was an optional choice, not an imperative." That those colonies who so chose to form themselves into a more perfect union did so willingly remains a testament to their optimism, courage, and collective resolve. But to achieve independence and to secure a nation are two different things, and we need not look long at the historical record to recognize how precarious can be the fortunes of a people thus born. That early Americans so quickly identified themselves as citizens of a self-constituted union is owing in large measure to the efforts of their early leaders. Jefferson was not alone engaged in this work, but he gave to the task a distinctive brand of thinking, a way of conceptualizing and expressing the values requisite to national identity. This thought, Bonwick explains, typically took as its referent the people, the federal government, and the states, and these in turn may be said to represent the basis of Jefferson's nationalism. The point is useful for our purposes because it draws attention to the complex play of forces that shaped the new president's vision, especially as they bore on the vexed issue of the preferred relationship between the states, the people, and their union.[41]

The first inaugural address was, in the words of Peter Onuf, "first and foremost an affirmation of American national identity, predicated on shared principles and bonds of affection and interest." The problem for Jefferson as for all Americans was that such bonds could never be assumed; at times in fact it was not at all clear that in so diverse a nation affections and interests could extend beyond individuals, families, and groups to states—much less to a distant and abstract entity called the Union. As we have seen, Jefferson had recourse to a theory of moral sentiment in which people were held to compose themselves naturally into social alliance. But the theory said nothing about specific political arrangements, and was in any case of limited application when it came to defending the tenets of republican government from its enemies. For Jefferson to affirm American national identity, he needed rather to articulate principles known, agreed on, and embedded in the national charter. Chief among these he professed absolute commitment to the concept of the federated union.[42]

At first glance the point seems perhaps redundant, for what is nationalism except allegiance to the nation? We need however only to recall the context of the inaugural ceremonies to appreciate the resonance of Jefferson's appeal to "State governments in all their rights" and to "the General government in its whole constitutional vigor." Jefferson was almost always confident, almost never complacent; and he long harbored doubts that others could prove themselves as steadfast as necessary to cement republican government. As late as August of 1800, Jefferson despaired of those who would, like certain New Englanders, persist in challenging the national covenant. Should they "continue in opposition to these principles of government, either knowingly or through delusion," Jefferson warned, "our government will be a very uneasy one. It can never be harmonious and solid, while so respectable a portion of it's [sic] citizens support principles which go directly to a change of the federal constitution, to sink the state governments, consolidate them into one, and to monarchize that."[43]

Jefferson hoped to dispel such delusion by underscoring the logic with which the states and union were united. The constitution in his view clearly implied that "the states are independent as to everything

within themselves, and united as to everything respecting foreign nations. Let the general government be reduced to foreign concerns only,
and let our affairs be disentangled from those of all other nations, except as to commerce." Here then was the true ground of national co-
mity: a free people pursuing their collective happiness, "hooped" by a
shared faith in the people's capacity to govern themselves, protected by
the national government from foreign incursions, but otherwise unfettered by centralized authority. The contest between state and union
was thus no contest at all, a false dichotomy urged by those who failed
to see the essential harmony inhering in the constitutional design. There
was in principle no reason that even so extensive an empire as Jefferson
dreamed could not flourish, however distant and different its federal
components. Altogether, he informed Gerry, the union thus conceived
was "the last anchor of our hope, and that alone which is to prevent
this heavenly country from becoming an arena of gladiators."[44]

Taken together, Jefferson's promotion of an expanding republican
empire, his insistence that America remain free from foreign entangle-
ments and unwarranted commercial restrictions, and his loyalty to
constitutional settlement cohere into a unified vision for national
strength. On reflection, we can see that, as Tucker and Hendrickson
suggest, Jefferson wished "that America could have it both ways—that
it could enjoy the fruits of power without falling victim to the normal
consequence of its exercise. He had good reasons for wanting both of
these things," they conclude, "because both were indispensable to the
realization of his vision of the American future." And what a vision it
was! To the Europeans he promised to "cultivate peace and commerce
with all." To his countrymen he declared that a prosperous peace was
the "only legitimate object of government, and the first duty of governors, and not the slaughter of men and devastation of the countries
placed under their care." And to those in the West awaiting the full blessings of republican government? He considered "their happiness as
bound up together, and that every measure" would be "taken which
may draw the bands of union tighter." The vision was exalted, the sentiment generous, the means uncertain: but it was nothing if not
Jefferson's own. In it can be glimpsed that embracing optimism

distinctive of his thought and language, expressed here by the mutually reinforcing dynamics of American nationhood: expanding but re-
taining its ideological integrity; neutral but advantageously integrated
into the world economy; federated but unified by the bonds of a shared
idea.[45]

These dynamics are explicitly on display in the inaugural address.
There we find evidence aplenty of Jefferson's "propensity to make of
every particular controversy the raw matter for a general theme transcending the immediate occasion, his genius at reducing a tangled problem of foreign diplomacy or domestic policy to an expression of such
simplicity and elegance that it immediately fixed itself on the popular
mind and became the 'tocsin of party.'" Part of this simplicity and elegance, we recall, is a result of Jefferson's habit of posing American and
European experiences in stark contrast; here, too, we see in the address
a characteristic mode of reasoning. In particular, the text evinces a
determined effort to pose the one against the other—not so much as
enemies but as one nation literally leaving the others behind. This rendering takes the form of a series of juxtaposed allusions, each one of
which sets in relief the opposition assumed to distinguish America from
her Old World progenitors.[46]

Jefferson's nationalism, we have noted, is predicated on the view that
America is destined to expand her republican domain, that she is like
no other nation on earth, and that she alone finds guidance in the
strength of constitutional republicanism. These tenets will represent
the positive terms of the text's contrast. Conversely, Jefferson depicts
Old World traditions, its current affairs and prospects, as the negative
counterpart to the meaning of America. Hence on the theme of imperial expansion: Jefferson's America is "a rising nation, spread out over a
wide and fruitful land, traversing all the seas with the rich productions
of industry, engaged in commerce with nations who feel power and
forget right, advancing rapidly to destinies beyond the reach of mortal
eye," a land so large, so bountiful, as to promise "room enough for our
descendants to the thousandth and thousandth generation." All this, it
bears reminding, without appeal to arms. Such imperial energies stand
in conspicuous contrast to European nations, who appear in the text

as historical abortions, exhausted, dead or dying principalities trapped in interminable cycles of violence and unchecked power. Where America had cleared the stage of false obstructions, Europe labored by sentiments "under which mankind has so long bled and suffered"; her past was marked by "throes and convulsions," the "agonizing spasms of infuriated man, seeking though blood and slaughter his long-lost liberty." The nation was thus for Jefferson more than a political category; it represented the vindication of history itself, a promise on the way to fulfillment that liberty could find a home, far away from the tyrannies of the past and the Old World and spreading ever westward.

The American penchant for viewing their country as a beacon unto the world is notorious, no less so because its august founders were most given to the boast. There is a difference, however, between mere chauvinism and recognizing that certain values seem especially well-expressed by a given political arrangement. Clearly Jefferson believed with many others that America had been providentially blessed. At the same time, he saw no reason in principle why the republican experiment might not be reproduced elsewhere; indeed that was the basic motive driving his "empire for liberty." At the moment, in any case, it seemed self-evidently true that the new nation exemplified its republican virtues like no other. Jefferson accordingly seizes upon the occasion of his inaugural the opportunity to proclaim America's exceptionalism.

In view of the nation's marginal status with respect to the European powers, her fledgling government and tiny military, the optimism coded into the speech might seem excessive even for Jefferson. The "world's best hope"? The "strongest government on earth"? If the claims here are not delusional, that is because Jefferson was above all a moralist, and he based his convictions not on conventional measures of age, population, or military might but the values upon which the nation defined itself. Those values—freedom, equality, virtue—he took to be the ground and height of republican government, and no other country could lay claim to them as could America. The inaugural address foregrounds this sense of distinction by posing against it a one-dimensional and undifferentiated image of Old World politics. Europe in the speech goes unnamed, as does France and England. That which is other than America is merely an abstraction, a distant and moot reality from long ago and far away. Jefferson's art in this context is implicative: it expresses a nationalism so convinced of its native identity that foreign powers scarcely bear mention, and even then only in the most indirect and cryptic terms. The Other: "nations who feel power and forget right"; "a troubled world"; "strangers"; "the ancient world"; "one quarter of the globe." Theorists of rhetoric teach us that every process of identification presupposes an equivalent process of differentiation. Here Jefferson bears out the principle with considerable skill, as if conducting a subtle movement in which America advances front and center to a stage otherwise dimmed, presenting finally an image of the nation in all its unique and manifest glory.

Conclusion

We have sought in this chapter to discern the rudiments of Jefferson's nationalist thought in general and as it appears in the inaugural address. To that end, I have admittedly asked that we place Jefferson in a role—as a political theorist—he would probably have resisted. Jefferson did not think of himself as a theorist, and certainly claimed no unique insight into the ways of mind and politics. These he drew from others, happy to apply their ideas to truths already well-established and widely, if loosely, understood by his countrymen. Still, the overall coherence of his thinking is evident in his appeal to the moral sense and the politics through which that sense finds expression, and we discover in the inaugural address a clear summation of his nationalist convictions. As a kind of political performance, his "system" appears to be well-conceived, strategic but responsible, idealistic but grounded in the exigencies of time and place.

That there were and remain limits to his thought is indisputable: observers then and now have taught us much about the various inconsistencies that plague even his most exalted production; the blithe opportunism he could display when reaching for justification; the systematic exclusion from membership in the "empire of liberty" of those deemed unfit. Jefferson, it must be said, reached far to conceive of a new and radically different future for his country; that he did not reach far enough is equally evident to our eyes. However exalted his nationalism, it could not, in the end, survive the internal tensions that ruptured the union a half-century later. No wonder, as recent scholars have noted, "ambivalence and qualification now surround most of his writings," and that he finally "has come to symbolize America's struggle with racial inequality." This much and more must be acknowledged as characteristic of the man and his vision. On the other hand, there can be no gainsaying the extent and sweep of that vision, a resolute faith, as James Truslow Adams wrote, "in the latent honesty and ability of the honest man, of man as man, regardless of social position, education, wealth, or other opportunities." At its best, Jefferson's dream was destined to inspire generations of Americans. And little wonder there either, for as Abraham Lincoln declared on the eve of his own revolution, "the principles of Jefferson are the definitions and axioms of a free society."[47]

CHAPTER 3

"The Circle of Our Felicities"

Rhetorical Dimensions of the First Inaugural Address

Thomas Jefferson was at length elected president of the United States of America on February 17, 1801. That left, even for his rapid pen, precious little time to compose what was to become, in Fawn Brodie's words, "one of the great seminal papers in American political history." Public anticipation of the inaugural day had been great, but it was scarcely all positive; in Burlingham, New Jersey, one embittered Federalist disabled a churchbell so as to prevent its ringing in Jefferson's new administration. Still, neither this nor any other such gestures of disappointment could dispel the more pervasive air of joy and relief that swept across the states. Indeed Jefferson's election was heralded with a degree of pomp second only to that accorded the illustrious Washington. Celebrants sang in the streets of "The People's Friend" ("What joyful prospects rise before / Peace, Arts, and Science hail our shore / Long may these blessings be preserv'd / And by a virtuous land deser'd / With JEFFERSON our head"). In Philadelphia, the *Aurora* reported, "The elegant schooner, 'Thomas Jefferson,' attracted a marked degree of attention from an admiring multitude—she was well officered, and manned by a crew of brave tars, accompanied by a number of that respectable and useful class of citizens, the ship-builders." For twelve dollars, supporters might purchase from George Helmold a "full length portrait of 'The Man of the People'," suitably "framed and glassed in a style of neatness and elegance." As for the inaugural address itself, copies could be ordered from Matthew Carey, "on satin, at different prices, from one dollar and quarter to one dollar and three quarters, according the quality of the satin."[1]

Those without the means to avail themselves of such luxuries could and did simply pick up a newspaper; there they might read not only Mr. Jefferson's speech but a good deal of commentary about it. Virtually all coverage of the event included mention of the "literary" or rhetorical character of the new president's performance. For some observers, it was Jefferson's famed skill in squeezing much thought into little space that impressed most, this being, as the *Independent Chronicle* noted, "the particular happiness attached to Mr. Jefferson's literary performances." Even a rock-ribbed New Hampshirite, not ordinarily given to such concessions, acknowledged in the *United States Oracle* that "every man of classic taste, must admit, that he is one of the best writers which our country has produced. The speech . . . considered in relation to its language, its perspicuity, its arrangement, its felicity of thought and expression, is most certainly a model of eloquence." The pity, wrote "Leonidas," was that Jefferson's own newspaper hacks were unable to follow their hero's example. "If they really admire Mr. Jefferson," he jibed, "let them, if they are capable of it, imitate the decorum of its language and moderation of his temper."[2]

The processions, songs, prints, speeches, and publications that welcomed Jefferson to the new century remind us that he was as much a product of his time as he was its architect. For all the boasting of republican simplicity, of Spartan austerity and native reserve, Americans were in truth a very noisy, literate, and publicly minded lot; enamored of ritual, inveterate readers of newspapers, pamphlets, and other prints; hungry for the spoken word whatever its form. This was, in short, a period of remarkable rhetorical energy, abetted by expanding print technologies, interest in the arts, educational growth, and literary production. Above all, it was an age when eloquence mattered, when the ability to speak and write powerfully about the common good was taken very seriously indeed. That ability was understood to be nothing less than an expression of republican virtue itself, a quality of leadership upon which depended the success of the new nation. As Robert Ferguson succinctly puts the point, "The republic's leaders fought constantly but not over the importance of public expression. To men of letters the message was the same regardless of party. Their place was the podium; their vehicle, the speech." We cannot, accordingly, fully grasp the meaning, force, and legacy of Jefferson's first inaugural address without considering in some detail its status as a rhetorical performance. Here it may be worth stressing again that in doing so, we do not place the speech over or against its partisan or theoretical purposes; it is rather to examine the ways in which those purposes are given their optimal expression.[3]

In this chapter, we seek to recover the full rhetorical resonance of Jefferson's address first by locating it within traditions of eighteenth-century rhetorical practice. On that general basis, we move then to examine the determinants of what might be called the Jeffersonian style, especially as that quality, strangely conspicuous *and* elusive, may be discerned in several of his earlier productions. We then take up a close examination of the inaugural speech and observe the ways in which this style is given its full rhetorical force. The chief aim of this chapter is to demonstrate that Jefferson's address can be explained by identifying the cultural energies circulating through the text without losing sight of its distinctive artistic achievement. And that achievement, again, was the full integration of the partisan, theoretical, and rhetorical into one of the nation's great texts of republican government.

Late in November of 1808, the president sat down to offer some advice to his grandson, Thomas Jefferson Randolph. The elder Jefferson was in a reflective mood, as might be expected under the circumstances: with two terms in office drawing to a close, a nation expanding at a breathtaking rate, and a private future ahead of him at last, grandfather Jefferson had much to offer in the way of retrospection. Recalling that, unlike his young correspondent, he had as a youth been thrown largely upon his own intellectual and moral resources, Jefferson gratefully acknowledged his "good fortune to become acquainted very early with some characters of very high standing, and to feel the incessant wish that I could even become what they were." These characters of standing—William Small, George Wythe, Peyton Randolph—remained for Jefferson exemplary voices, models of wisdom to whom he might look as he faced the real choices in life. Among these choices involved the matter of reputation: which kind did he prefer? "That of a horse jockey? A foxhunter? An Orator? Or the honest advocate of my country's rights?" That Jefferson should place orators in the same category as horse jockeys and fox hunters is telling in its own right; the sentiment is expressed even more pointedly, however, as he proceeds to lay down a series of prudential rules for his grandson's consumption. Among these, Jefferson stresses, "I must not omit the important one of never entering into dispute or argument with another. I never yet saw an instance of one of two disputants convincing the other by argument. I have seen many on their getting warm, becoming rude, and shooting one another." Conviction was to be secured not through such exchanges nor in such heat, Jefferson wrote, but was instead "the effect of our own dispassionate reasoning, either in solitude, or weighing within ourselves dispassionately what we hear from others standing uncommited in argument ourselves."[4]

Jefferson's reflections help introduce and shape our thinking about his rhetorical legacy in several ways. At one level, the sensibility they express is consistent with an enduring version of the man: contemplative, statesmanlike, above or at least outside the bumptious scenes of political wrangling—in short, the rhetorical equivalent to the nonpartisan Jefferson. This is the Jefferson of few words but many thoughts, the Sage of Monticello, coming to conviction in dispassionate solitude. We need not dwell on this image for long before we see how peculiar it really is, how strangely Jefferson's words and our willingness to take them on face value have refracted attention away from the more complex, more interesting, certainly more engaged Jefferson. This is the partisan leader, the polemical spokesman for colonial rights, the drafter of resolutions and declarations, statutes of freedom and responses to imperious ministers. Here is the rhetorical Jefferson who, far from meditating at cool remove was very much in the heat of virtually every important contest of the nation's first years. Coming to terms with this

Jefferson, this enormously talented disputant who would lump orators with sportsmen, will be an important first step toward understanding his inaugural address in all its rhetorical complexity.

Perhaps the surest route to the rhetorical basis of Jefferson's thought is, so to speak, through his library door. Inside, we find several kinds of evidence suggestive of what in his lifetime Jefferson probably read and thought about the arts of rhetoric and oratory. Some of these works will be discussed in greater detail, and we shall defer the subject of oratory to a different section; but we may observe at least the following. First, as student first of the College of William and Mary (1760–62) and thereafter of law (1762–65), Jefferson was read and practiced in rhetorical theory; indeed the William Small to whom he referred so affectionately many years later in the letter to his grandson occupied the college's Professorship in Ethics, Rhetoric, and Belles Lettres. In his autobiography, Jefferson recalled many years later that Small was "a man profound in most of the useful branches of science, with a happy talent of communication, correct and gentlemanly manners, and an enlarged and liberal mind . . . and from his conversation I got my first views of the expansion of science and of the system of things in which we are placed." Under his welcome influence the young Jefferson would have been exposed most likely to major figures in the classical and neo-classical rhetorical traditions, as well as to more recent and innovative works on the subject. Here was a mind, in any case, formed and cultivated early in the craft of persuasive speech.[5]

A second glance at Jefferson's writings reveals that not only was he a beneficiary of such education, but that he sought to pass on its lessons—in some cases quite literally—to younger aspirants for distinction. Jefferson was characteristically generous when it came to requests for advice on such matters as the proper course of study for law or learning generally, and he was nothing if not systematic. We thus have as accurate a record as we might wish for what he thought was important to the intellectual and professional development of a young man. Virtually all such advice included the names and titles of prominent works in rhetoric and closely associated disciplines. To Bernard Moore, Jefferson (himself still at study of law), recommended a notably strict routine of daily and evening readings. "From Dark to Bedtime," the presumably indefatigable Mr. Moore was to read in "Belles Lettres; Criticism; Rhetoric; and Oratory," including Shakespeare, Kames's *Elements of Criticism,* Hugh Blair's *Rhetoric,* and Thomas Sheridan's *A Course of Lectures on Elocution.* In 1771 Jefferson again offered his help on such matters, this time to his brother-in-law Robert Skipworth, who had requested a catalogue of essential books; among them, Jefferson includes Kames's *Elements,* Burke's *Philosophical Inquiry into the Origins of Our Ideas of the Sublime and Beautiful,* Adam Smith's *Theory of Moral Sentiments,* and Cicero's *De oratore* and *Tusculan Disputations.* And when, as Jefferson set out imagining his ideal university, "where every branch of science, deemed useful at this day, should be taught it its highest degree," he envisioned a curriculum that included among its core disciplines Belles Lettres, Rhetoric, and Oratory—to be superintended by one of the university's six "Professorships."[6]

And then there is the library itself, Jefferson's own repository of learning and gift ultimately to the Library of Congress. A good deal has been written about this near-mythic collection, and in mentioning certain of its volumes here we need to be mindful that they are, like those previously noted, but a few of a relatively comprehensive set of titles in the sciences, religion, history, philosophy, and the fine arts. Still it is worth noting for the purposes of this chapter, where Jefferson is to be viewed as a rhetorical artist preeminently, that no less than thirty-three titles are explicitly the concern of rhetoric and oratory, an even dozen treating of rhetoric exclusively. They are about evenly divided between classical and eighteenth-century treatises, and include such notable works as Aristotle's *Rhetoric,* Cicero's *De oratore,* Quintilian's *Institutes,* John Ward's *A System of Oratory,* Blair's *Lectures,* and Sheridan's *Elocution.* Clearly we have in Jefferson a thinker, writer, and speaker who remained invested his entire adult life in the art of rhetoric. His own education trained him to this appetite, he saw such knowledge as important to be passed on to others through future generations, and he gave its literature a place in his cherished library.[7]

Even so brief a review suggests that the case against a view of Jefferson as hostile to rhetoric may be readily summoned. But we are still left with a lingering image of a figure reticent and ill-suited to public debate, and at the same time a highly accomplished polemical stylist, a political thinker who gave to his ideas lasting force. Perhaps we have an enigma here only, another mysterious feature of Jefferson's personality that might just as well be entered into the register of his other paradoxical traits. I think not, if only because the disjunctions noted are not so mysterious as all that. A more refined conception of what we are talking about when we talk about rhetoric—and Jefferson's relationship to that art—will largely dissolve the problem. A number of observations suggest themselves: as with parties, Jefferson knew he could not, despite his protests, do without arguments and arguing; a good many effective communicators are more at ease with a pen than with a podium—and vice versa; to hold out standards of oratorical display more appropriate to the age of Calhoun, Webster, and Clay is to seriously misapply those standards to Jefferson's time; and, in any case, Jefferson's alleged disaffection for public speech, if true, was perfectly in keeping with a model of decorum embodied in none other than the redoubtable George Washington.

All of this said, we have available a more positive and systematic approach toward recovering the rhetorical foundations of Jefferson's thought. That work can begin by recognizing that, as in his thinking generally, Jefferson was more ecumenical than systematic; he exercised his great reading and restless imagination upon those sources which offered the most for the purposes at hand. Perhaps he was well-read in rhetorical theory, perhaps not; but he was certainly a very keen observer of how people acted upon their theoretical precepts. In any case, it is highly unlikely that he ever saw the need or merit in systematically integrating a particular body of rhetorical principles into his own rhetorical practice. If his debt to rhetorical thought may be identified, it rests in the selective appropriation of certain standards associated with classical, contemporary, and elocutionary developments. Certain scholars, chief among them Wilbur Samuel Howell, Jay Fliegelman, and Sandra Gustafson, are more inclined than others to stress a direct relationship between Jefferson's rhetorical practice and specific developments in eighteenth-century rhetorical theory. There is advantage in this, and because I will not be taking it with respect to the first inaugural address a brief explanation is perhaps due the reader.[8]

While it is the case that Jefferson no doubt studied some rhetoric and belles lettres under Professor Small, as we have noted, and that his library contained a number of volumes on the subject, it is not nearly as evident that he studied these works seriously in his maturity, that he took their prescriptions to heart or was in any significant way influenced by one school of rhetorical thought or the other. Even if we can observe certain qualities of his prose that accord with the precepts of a given body of rhetorical theory, say its widely acclaimed perspicuity, it does not follow that such a relationship affords much explanatory weight; indeed it would be the rare (and obscure) author who did not exercise such rhetorical virtues. To put the matter otherwise: seeking to explain the distinctive properties of Jefferson's inaugural with reference to contemporary theory would seem no more promising than interpreting Lincoln's Gettysburg address in view of nineteenth-century textbooks on rhetoric and oratory. Either performance might illustrate this or that rhetorical norm, but then what? We will have rather missed the bigger and more important picture by remanding them to the province of manuals designed for schoolboys and pedagogues.

By way of an alternative, the approach undertaken here stresses instead a view of Jefferson's address as representing itself on its own terms. The central claim driving such an orientation is that he sought to activate through his performance the specific partisan and philosophical principles detailed in the preceding chapters. From these principles Jefferson took his inspiration, purpose, and design. The first inaugural address is accordingly seen best as a conspicuous display of its author's style and thought; it is in this context a statement about what oratory ought to look and sound like to a nation of republicans. A speech about politics, it offers as well a politics of speech; it is a rhetorical expression of the republican creed, and the republican expression of a rhetorical creed. The first inaugural address thus constitutes its own theory of rhetoric; it is an exemplification of republican virtue, the conception, design, and delivery of which was meant to instantiate Jefferson's vision of a new moral and political order.

So much is not to suggest, of course, that the first inaugural address, for all its singularity, was sui generis. It is to suggest that we might well look elsewhere than to conventional rhetoric manuals alone as a means of giving it context and location within the cultural moment in which it was delivered. This context is appropriately the rhetorical milieu of late eighteenth-century America, the robust and energetic environment of public speech, debate, sermonizing and pamphleteering that helped define the political life of the early republic. Here we will find our ingress, our route toward a fuller explication of the inaugural text. Such an approach grants us a degree of intimacy and association that theoretical abstractions cannot; it gives us access to voices and personalities, lived experiences and popular sentiments that go far toward helping us understand the immediate and enduring circumstances of the address. In the following, some of the more significant features of this rhetorical culture are briefly discussed as a way of framing the more detailed work of the subsequent textual analysis.

Rhetorical Contexts

History reveals to us time and again how interlocked are the fortunes of democracy and the arts of persuasion. From antiquity to the present, the health of one remains in no small measure a function of the other: as the polity goes, so goes rhetoric. Americans of the eighteenth and nineteenth centuries knew as much, indeed reflected a good deal on this persistent but quite fragile relationship. "The experience of the world has shown pretty conclusively," observed the *North American Review,* "that eloquence and political liberty go hand in hand, flourish under similar favoring influences, and, dying together, are buried in the same grave." Looking back over the nation's first century of existence, the writer confidently surmised that both liberty and eloquence were given new life, meaning, and energy in republican America, with all its "links of electric sympathy between the patriot speaker and the tumultuous assemblages of free and sovereign citizens, gathered to consider questions of moment to the public weal, or to celebrate, with the pomp of solemn processions, religious rites, and commemorative orations, the illustrious achievements of the mighty dead, to call up the famous days which have been turning points in the history of national greatness." Pride so confident may be appreciated ironically for having been expressed a decade before the Civil War. But it may just as well remind us that the symbiosis thought to animate the political and the rhetorical was never taken for granted, indeed revisited most frequently at moments of greatest uncertainty.[9]

To grasp the achievement of Jefferson's first inaugural address is to acknowledge what the "experience of the world" confirms, that eloquence and liberty either flourish together or, "dying together, are buried in the same grave." The proximity of this relationship suggests that what is observed of one term ought to be observed of the other, as in fact we must in reference to Jefferson's address. That is to say, the qualities attributable to political life in the 1790s and in the first years of the new century find their analogue in the rhetorical practices through which that life was mediated. The instability, the heat, the apparently boundless energies, the push and pull of tradition and novelty, the dialectics of expansion and retraction—all characteristic, too, of the rhetorical dynamics shaping and given shape by political developments. As a preliminary for our reading of the inaugural address, this interplay of the political and the rhetorical is best comprehended as a description of public life generally, where rapid transformation in the social, economic, and cultural factors making up that life set the stage for Jefferson's "revolution." Historians continue to debate the precise sources, meaning, and consequences of the period, but all agree that the "first generation of Americans," as Joyce Appleby subtitles a recent work, effected powerful new realities on the shared lives of citizens throughout the republic.[10]

Two such realities are especially pertinent here. First, the unprecedented expansion of the spaces of political action drastically transformed the opportunities for those already or newly enfranchised to let their voices be heard. "The frothy political discourses," Appleby writes, "the marketing of printed material, and the enlarged circle of readers worked together to make publicity the shaping force in the political realm." Second, and by direct implication, this unleashing of popular power became at once the source and object of public opinion formation. Citizens and their leaders knew themselves to be in a different world than that which obtained before the Revolution; certain continuities were still evident, of course, but the sheer fact of a new and formidable type—the American citizen—asserted itself with unmistakable force. Political activity, as a result, and the rhetorical labor required to organize this new creature "public opinion," changed for good (or ill, depending on how one viewed the prospects of a government of, by, and for the people). "The Revolution," Gordon Wood explains, "rapidly expanded this 'public' and democratized its opinion. Every conceivable form of printed matter—books, pamphlets, handbills, posters, broadsides, and especially newspapers—multiplied and were now written and read by many more ordinary people than ever before in history."[11]

A new nation, a literate and politically engaged public, a president whose very identity announced the triumph of republican values upon and for which independence was fought and gained: here was a combination of novelties bound to enthral or terrify. But of course no generation is ever born entirely anew, no revolution so complete as to wipe out all precedent. And this is true no less for the rhetorical culture of the new republic than for its attendant political life. Just as certain principles and practices of the latter continued to make themselves felt under the new order, so the former continued to shape the nation's discursive habits. Jefferson's inaugural, like his politics, was at once forward-looking and indebted to certain rhetorical traditions, and by looking at those traditions, we can situate it where it rightfully belongs—at the cusp, between the eighteenth and nineteenth centuries, between the old and new. To this end, the following briefly examines three conventions of public discourse—religious, civic, and political—that in general ways shaped the address, its reception, and its legacy.

RELIGIOUS CONTEXTS

Any attempt to situate Jefferson's address in relation to the religious culture of his time may well seem misguided from the outset. Readers familiar with his reputation as an inveterate enemy of sectarianism, his work on behalf of religious freedom, and his notorious indifference to institutionalized Christianity are apt to dismiss, indeed ignore, Jefferson's debt to the rhetorical conventions shaping the religious life of the new republic. At the personal level, to be sure, we must be very careful in attributing to his thought anything like a coherent or neatly packaged set of religious convictions. Jefferson was deeply skeptical about the probity of organized Christianity, and there can be no gainsaying his fierce resistance to those who would return his new country back into the hands of a discredited religious elite. Jefferson the man was in fact much concerned about matters of faith and divinity; Jefferson the politician was adamant not to have his or anyone else's religious convictions intrude into the affairs of state.[12]

On what basis, then, can it be said that his inaugural address in part owed its character, its rhetorical power, in some measure to the religious culture of the period? The answer must be pitched at a rather broad level, and no effort will be made here to link specific words with specific doctrine; that is not how this speech—nor or any inaugural address for that matter—functions rhetorically. Jefferson rather sought to give his words their most general application and their broadest possible scope; in this, he fully appreciated the fact that Americans were a people deeply, in some ways definitively, religious. Again, such recognition presumed no uniformity of faith. Indeed it was precisely the fact that Americans were so diverse, sometimes at odds, sometimes losing and then regaining perspective that Jefferson appealed not to their differences but to what it was they held in common when it came to religious sentiment. In view of this challenge, Jefferson sought to effect in the first inaugural address what he previously had sought when composing the Declaration of Independence: "Not to find out new principles, or new arguments, never before thought of, not merely to say things which had never been said before; but to place before mankind the common sense of the subject, in terms so plain and firm as to command their assent. . . . Neither aiming at originality of principles or sentiments, nor yet copied from any particular and previous writing, it was intended to be an expression of the American mind, and to give to that expression the proper tone and spirit called for by the occasion."

When it came to the religious dimensions of "the American mind" Jefferson had before him a set of perfectly familiar and still-powerful thematics from which to draw. Among those figuring most prominently in the inaugural address are three propositions embraced by nearly all citizens: that Americans were a chosen people; that by virtue of that fact the nation was set on a path toward ever greater progress; and that to keep on this path Americans must undertake rituals of rededication and renewal.[13]

Whatever their creed, wherever they practiced it, and whenever they reflected on it, Americans had remained convinced that they were singular. Divine providence had ordained that this people, for all their faults, were possessed of a special mission and qualities of mind, body, and spirit alone up to the task of making the new world truly a New World. Almost two centuries earlier, John Winthrop had invoked on board the *Arabella* Matthew's faith "that we shall be as a city upon a hill" and warned too that the "eyes of all people are upon us." That conviction, that insistence for better or worse never failed to shape the colonists' sense of themselves and their role in the world. A nation now, Americans continued to thank God, in the words of Israel Evans, "by whose providential goodness and power the lines are fallen unto us in pleasant places; yea, we have a godly heritage. Here harvests grow for the free and cheerful husbandman: here, neither awed by lordly and rapacious injustice, nor dejected by beholding idleness high fed and fattened on the labors of other men, they reap and enjoy the pleasing fruits of their honest industry." Thus when Jefferson spoke during his inaugural of "the world's best hope," of "the strongest Government on earth," of "possessing a chosen country, with room enough for our descendants to the thousandth and thousandth generation," he spoke in a language of abiding and peculiar power. Federalists and republicans, Puritan and deist, rich and poor, Yankee and Cavalier: all could see an image of themselves written into this twice-told tale of America as a chosen people.[14]

A chosen people, Jefferson and his audience knew, was an active people. Fleeing persecution and finding freedom, the early colonists had only begun to realize the full responsibility and the full prospect before them. Because they were select, they were bound in covenant, and that covenant bound all Americans to the cultivation and increase of the bounty God had bestowed. The rewards, as Samuel Danforth reminded his congregants, were as great as the labor required to summon them forth: "Attend we are Errand," Danforth promised, "upon which Christ sent us into the Wilderness, and he will provide Bread for us." At the dawn of a new century it seemed to many Americans that providence had more than made good on that promise; progress was evident everywhere, and was this not proof positive that the new nation had in fact secured the full blessings of liberty? "We possess an extensive, noble country," declared Samuel Miller in a sermon of 1793. "Fertility and beauty vie with each other, in favor of our ease, accommodation, and delight. Every avenue to national importance, and the felicity of individuals, is opened wide. Let it then, in addition to all these advantages, and to complete its glory, let it be Immanuel's land. This will render you at once the pattern," Miller told his listeners, "and the wonder of the world." Jefferson no less than the Presbyterian minister was enthralled by what he saw before him, "A rising nation, spread over a wide and fruitful land, traversing all the seas with the rich productions of their industry . . . advancing rapidly to destinies beyond the reach of mortal eye." All this, Jefferson and his audience knew, was the just reward due a people chosen by a "Providence, which by all its dispensations proves that it delights in the happiness of man here and his greater happiness hereafter." Surely even the most inveterate critic of Jefferson's religious views would be hard put to deny his or her own place in such a scheme of things.[15]

Jefferson was known in his own time as he is in ours as the consummate optimist. This quality, so apparent throughout his writings, in no small degree accounts for his popularity then and his enduring appeal ever since. Indeed it has been transcribed onto the American spirit itself, as if in Jefferson's unfailing hopes for republican government we might find the self-flattering reflection of our own boundless faith in American destiny. But faith, religious, political, or otherwise, requires labor. This much Jefferson understood keenly. The inaugural address was in fact part of this labor, a work designed to shore up confidence, assuage anxieties, keep his audience on that path pointing so auspiciously to the future. Recalling again that this was but the fourth such inaugural address of the new nation, we can appreciate the imperative under which this task was undertaken: When the object of faith is so new, so alone in the world, what rituals of rededication are necessary to remind this people of their special role and retain their confidence in the rewards that surely lie ahead? For all its novelty, Jefferson's address was recognizable as a ritualized performance crafted specifically to strengthen collective resolve; it accordingly participated in a venerable tradition of religious discourse focused on just this challenge. Again, this is not to imply that Jefferson was self-consciously patterning his language on such discourse or on any special strain within it. It is to alert us to the common and nearly universal function of rhetoric to rededicate common values and mutual commitment to each other's fortunes.

Jefferson's audience that day was heir to a longstanding, diverse, and still-resonant tradition of such rituals, ranging from fast day and artillery sermons to prayers of thanksgiving. The key to these rituals was their binding together again a people at peril, to forge again a commanding rationale for standing together with faces turned courageously toward the future. Thus Jonathan Mayhew steadied his audience during the Stamp Act crisis by insisting that it was "most prudent, most christian, to bury in oblivion what is past; to begin our civil, political life anew as it were, from this joyful and glorious era of restored and confirmed liberty; to be at union among ourselves; to abstain from all party names and national reflections, respecting any of our fellow subjects, and to exert ourselves, in our several stations, to promote the common good, by 'love serving one another.'" These and countless sermons throughout the founding era attest to a telling combination of optimism and anxiety about the American errand; rhetorically, they functioned to restore a faith already strong but always exposed to doubt; to reunite a people destined to move forward but given to laxity and bouts of disorientation; to remind citizens, as did David Tappan in his 1792 election sermon, to be "just and kind to one another, united and jealously attached to the great interests of America, and of the whole human fraternity. Then we shall hold out an inviting example to all the world," Tappan said, "of the propitious operation of a free government; we shall encourage and accelerate the progress of reason, and of liberty, through the globe." Like Tappan, Mayhew, and many other leaders before him, Jefferson availed himself in 1801 of a rich storehouse of experiences and symbols from the American religious tradition. From that tradition, he found one way, at least, to "look with encouragement for that guidance and support which may enable us to steer with safety the vessel in which we are all embarked amidst the conflicting elements of a troubled world."[16]

CIVIC COMMEMORATION

As broad and deep as such religious tradition was in the early republic, it was but a part of a more general and complex rhetorical culture. Closely related to it was an equally vibrant set of conventions associated with rituals of civic commemoration. Americans then as now were tireless workers of public memory, bent, it often seems, on fixing every glance toward the future from coordinates set by the past. The many occasions and motives through which such celebrations were mediated meant that the arts of civic commemoration could not be limited to a specific genre or rhetorical type; not oratory alone but any number of symbolic practices were set in motion to assist in bringing history into the national present. Songs, poetry, monuments, essays, painting, and public speech all helped to turn the past into a spectacle for the education, entertainment, and aspirations of the new republic. Taken together, all these forms represented a loose but powerful chain with which Americans bound themselves locally and nationally as citizens of one country. The productions flowing from these occasions may strike us now as mere ephemera, but it is a mistake to discount their centrality to the labor of citizenship. They are, as David Waldstreicher has argued, definitively "nationalist practices, every bit as much as the processions they announced, punctuated, and described. They did more than spread nationalism," Waldstreicher notes, "they constituted a national popular political culture."[17]

The first inaugural address—singularly eloquent, so distinctively Jeffersonian—would seem far distant from the messier world of parades, toasts, and popular oratory. In many ways it is, of course, but in another sense Jefferson's masterpiece was shaped decisively by such ritualized rehearsals of nationhood. It was in no small part an artifact of a robust public culture; as a rhetorical performance, it thus relied for its intended effect on the habits and expectations of that culture. Whether or not they discerned in Jefferson's language the full range of its meaning, the people who heard or read the speech were well-positioned to recognize it for what it was and what it hoped to accomplish. What they perceived must have been reassuringly familiar: an event at once dignified but not excessively so; local in its delivery and source but reaching out to the nation as a whole; about political life but not overtly partisan. These were indeed the markers of many other such performances: the ubiquitous fourth of July oration, the annual celebrations of Washington's birthday, commencement day addresses. This was, certainly, an exemplary instance of civic commemoration, but it held in common with all such rituals the purpose of rallying citizens to the banner of republican government by appealing to a shared past, a collective identity, and a future befitting a free and united people. The first inaugural address was of a piece, a particularly striking instance of a process described by James Farrell as a national effort to "express the praise and admiration of celebrants for the noble deeds of American revolutionaries, to craft a useful history and consign those narratives to the public memory, to suggest a dominant national identity proud of its past and confident of its future, and to hold up models of civic virtue and patriotism to be emulated by future political and military leaders."[18]

If Jefferson's oration is to be regarded in part as participating in this more general context of civic commemoration, we need now to consider more specifically how these rituals took on their rhetorical force. If, that is to say, these rituals worked by staging the drama of nationhood, with what materials was that spectacle composed? How and to what effect was it so framed as to present in the most compelling terms possible the story of America and its victorious republican revolution? Three broad and clearly interdependent characteristics suggest themselves as answers to that question. At the local level, these rituals were presented as a kind of political theater, the chief function of which was to give to the occasion its maximum visual, auditory, and affective power; at the national level, this appeal was expanded and applied through developing technologies of print and reportage; and at the level of historical transformation, the rituals of nationhood extended their reach across generations to ensure the survival of a citizenry up to the task of self-government.

By way of perspective on just how theatrical public life could be in the early republic, we might recall the events surrounding the nation's first inaugural ceremonies. In April of 1789, George Washington was accompanied from Philadelphia to New York by a seemingly endless series of parades, orations, and pageantry. At one point, Charles Wilson Peel's daughter Angelica (in white robes) managed with the help of a special contraption to lower onto the new president's head a laurel crown as he passed onto a bridge into Philadelphia. Young Angelica's was but one of thousands of such gestures that swept Washington to his appointed speech in New York's Federal Hall. Nearing Trenton, he was greeted by girls (also in white) tossing flowers before him and singing "Virgins fair, and Matrons grave, / Those thy conquering arms did save / Build for these triumphal bowers / Strew, ye fair, his way with flowers / Strew your Hero's way with flowers."[19]

True, spectacle at this level could be appropriate to Washington alone, and Jefferson, it is safe to say, neither warranted nor expected any girls to guild his path with rose petals. In the event, his inauguration ceremonies were conspicuously simple; so much so, in fact, that his critics accused him of debasing the office. But the key word here is conspicuous, for Jefferson knew as well as anyone that the inauguration of power was above all a symbolic act, the meaning and force of which depended on what people actually saw, heard, and experienced. His own inauguration and the speech attending it were artfully rendered scenes in the drama that was republicanism. They were accordingly designed to impart the spectacle of dignity without monarchical trappings, to embody and enact that special virtue Americans claimed as their own.

Not everyone, of course, was fortunate enough to bear direct witness to such scenes. That all could learn of them from a distance was the result of a rapidly developing print culture that included newspapers, broadsides, pamphlets, and periodicals. Consequently, readers from Maine to Georgia and virtually everywhere in between learned of the day's events when, as Philadelphia's *Aurora* reported, "there appeared to be a calm and exquisite diffusion of delight—the cessation of party animosity was for a time complete, and from the tears which bedewed many manly cheeks, and union of opinion in applause, there appeared to be a total, and prospect of a perpetual annihilation of party passions." That much was optimistic, to be sure. Party passions erupted soon thereafter, and readers could gauge their own sentiments by tracking debates and commentary of newspapers throughout the states. "In Virginia," wrote one skeptic in the Charleston *Gazette*, "we are not so sanguine as you are, and we read the inaugural speech, without finding any thing in it to cherish the hopes of the friends of regular government, good order, and peace."[20]

The partisan energies driving the press at the time meant that whatever pretensions to being above party Jefferson may have had were quickly deflated. But the more general and relevant fact is that the press played a key role in sustaining the drama of politics and hence the life of the new nation. Put another way, print culture and reportage assisted directly in the process whereby a people distant to each other come to recognize themselves as fellow citizens; in the words of Benedict Anderson, they "gradually become aware of the hundreds of thousands, even millions, of people in their particular language-field, and at the same time that only those hundreds of thousands, or millions, so belonged. These fellow-readers, to whom they were connected through print, formed, in their secular, particular, visible invisibility, the embryo of the nationally imagined community."[21]

Both in the immediate experience of witnessing civic ceremony and in reading about it, Americans were fast moving from Anderson's embryonic stage toward greater levels of maturation. This was so in part because they were not *merely* witnessing such rituals of national affirmation as presidential inaugurations: they were actively participating in that very process. To do so, to be aware of national as well as local events, to read, perhaps even write an ode to virtue, to strew flowers, or to attend a fourth of July celebration was to act as a citizen of the republic. But the instantiation of republican virtue through these rituals required more even than attending or reading about them; it obliged all citizens to pass on their legacy of freedom to future generations. So obviously the beneficiaries of the struggle for republican government, Americans shouldered the responsibility to ensure against its demise by keeping its promises ever alive in the hearts and minds of those about to receive its blessings. Whether they participated in person or at a distance, celebrants were expected to somehow disseminate the experience of citizenship. This they did by establishing recurrent and regular celebrations of nationhood (eventually including Jefferson's own of March 4). It is central to our understanding of Jefferson's inaugural address and of the rhetorical culture to which it spoke that we see it in its ritualized aspect. A great deal of the rhetorical power of ritual is precisely its reproducibility; it can be observed time and again; it endures across state lines and partisan difference; it persists through generations to bind citizens together in history as well as place.

In a nation so young as Jefferson's, threatened within by party strife and without by foreign wars and intrigue, it would be nearly impossible to overstate the significance of these functions. Like the many other forms of civic ceremony to which it was related, the inaugural address as such provided a certain ballast against the waves of social change and political strife. It is crucial to recognize, moreover, that the stability purchased through ritual did not come at the cost of eliminating dissent; ballast only works when countered by competing forces. In this context we may observe that Jefferson's inaugural address works not in the absence of conflict but by virtue of it; that is in part its brilliance, as clear and compelling an example as could be got of Waldstreicher's keen insight: the remarkable thing about Jeffersonian Americans was that it fashioned such rituals "in order to have their partisanship with their nationalism, their *communitas* with their campaigning: to be local citizens and national subjects."[22]

POLITICAL DEBATE

The rhetorical culture of the new nation was textured in decisive and discernible ways by these traditions of religious and civic discourse.

Jefferson's inaugural address, while not wholly explicable with reference to these traditions alone, is not wholly explicable without them. Similarly, a third broad context bears directly on our understanding of the address, its sources, character, and legacy. For nearly half a century, public life in America had been defined and transformed by political disputation—unabashed, sometimes shrill, often eloquent—but resolutely polemical efforts to forge the national ethos. Much of this work, as we have seen, took its inspiration from certain religious and civic influences, and no effort will be made here to select out political debate as a separate rhetorical genre. At the same time, there is reason to acknowledge the role of an overtly political tradition of public "discussion"—the gloves-off, hard-hitting give-and-take of debate that made no attempt to mask its ambitions under the guise of religious or civic ritual. For evidence of this tradition we need not seek far: the rhetoric of nationhood is always a noisy affair, and as Bernard Bailyn dryly reminds us, reticence was not a problem for most Americans. Before the war, colonial leaders "wrote easily and amply, and turned out in the space of scarcely a decade and a half and from a small number of presses a rich literature of theory, argument, opinion, and polemic. Every medium of expression was put to use." If that was the case before independence, it was even more so afterward, and Jefferson figures very much as a leading voice in this already crowded and vocal life of the new republic.[23]

But how? If the inaugural address is to be situated within this tradition, in what ways specifically does it work its political ends? The question is more complex than it may appear at first glance, if only because Jefferson's own posture in the political wrangling of his time proved so paradoxical. As we have seen in chapter one, the first inaugural was at one level an intensely partisan document, evidence if any were needed that its author was a political animal of the most primal type. And, too, Jefferson had played a leading role at the avant-garde of radical politics for a quarter-century of American life; surely no further evidence need be summoned to establish his credentials as a disputant of the first order. At the same time, his inaugural address is notable as much for what it appears not to be as for what it actually is—a highly political expression of values that claim no partisan allegiances. Here we arrive at the nub of Jefferson's complex stance toward the rhetorical culture of which he was both a product and an enemy. Joseph Ellis's pointed comment captures nicely the point: "One of the reasons he [Jefferson] was so notoriously ineffective in debate was that argument itself offended him. The voices he heard inside himself were all harmonious and agreeable, reliable expressions of the providentially aligned universal laws that governed the world as he knew it, so that argument struck him as dissonant noise that defied the natural order of things."[24]

The quality of mind to which Ellis refers may be directly mapped onto the rhetorical quality of the inaugural address. It is, paradoxically, a performance born of political debate but designed to transcend it, fashioned by one of history's great polemicists, who at the same time was deeply distrustful of conflict. We should not be surprised, then, to see in its language the imprint of two tendencies, mutually at odds but coexisting by virtue of the rhetorical artistry it commands. We shall address these features in greater detail, but here, where we seek a general sense of how the inaugural may be placed in the context of eighteenth-century political debate, it will be worth noting several key markers. On the one hand, the speech works thematically by taking into itself many, perhaps most, of the commonplaces associated with revolutionary, constitutional, and early republican rhetoric. A quick list makes the point:

> *A rising nation spread over a wide and fruitful land*
> *engaged in commerce with nations who feel power*
>   *and forget right*
> *advancing rapidly to destinies beyond the reach of*
>   *mortal eye*
> *all will, of course, arrange themselves under the will*
>   *of the law*
> *and unite in common efforts for the common good*
> *the will of the majority is in all cases to prevail*
> *that will to be rightful must be reasonable*

the minority possess their equal rights
This government, the world's best hope
the strongest government on earth
possessing a chosen country
a wise and frugal Government
shall not take from the mouth of labor the bread it
  has earned
Equal and exact justice to all men
freedom of religion
freedom of the press
freedom of person
peace, liberty, and safety

What true republican could but applaud such principles? They are among those for which the revolution was fought and secured; to believe in them was to be an American. That these transcendent values were now in fact commonplaces was the result of a rhetorical process, a culture of debate and dissent that propelled thirteen colonies into nationhood. And here we gain our clue to the rhetorical ingenuity of Jefferson's address, for in appealing to that which all would agree, the speaker appealed to that which was now beyond debate and dissent, to the "creed of our political faith." Jefferson sought accordingly to speak to a citizenry for whom these verities were no longer at issue, no longer subject to dispute. His was an argument that presumed argument no longer necessary.

Finally, the status of Jefferson's speech as an *inaugural* address is an obvious but important clue to its meaning, shape, and delivery. To speak of such address as constituting a genre is perhaps overly generous: only three presidential inaugurations, after all, had been accompanied by the ritual of speech we have come to take for granted. As Stephen Lucas has pointed out, however, certain rhetorical antecedents can be traced to explain the distinctive form and content marking the inaugural address generally. Chief among these, Lucas notes, was the rhetoric of office evident in British and colonial tradition. Under these circumstances, "the new office-holder typically acknowledged the person or persons responsible for granting the office, noted the magnitude and/ or importance of the duties attached to that office, expressed humility about his capacity to carry out those duties, and pledged his utmost effort to meet his responsibilities ably and honorably." More specifi- cally, Lucas locates the template for early presidential inaugural ad- dresses in the office-taking rituals associated with the arrival of new governors to the Virginia Council and House of Burgesses. In these cases, Lucas writes, the governor "announced the general principles that would guide his administration, mentioned one or two issues of press- ing importance, praised the legislature for its knowledge, virtue, and loyalty, and urged that it avoid faction and promote the public weal in every respect." Jefferson's address unmistakably bears these antecedent imprints, and in recalling them we take one step further toward a full appreciation for how he realized the potential inherent to the form.[25]

Taken together, these religious, civic, and political traditions of rhe- torical discourse shaped Jefferson's first inaugural address in complex but recognizable ways. They remind us, too, that we have in that text evidence of an original mind and extraordinary stylist, even as that mind and that style is put to the task of rehearsing cultural truisms. To give singular expression to common values: that was Jefferson's rare gift. As we move closer to a more detailed examination of the text, it will prove useful to briefly recall how that gift was itself shaped and devel- oped through the author's personal engagement in his nation's found- ing. Turning to several of his most notable rhetorical performances previous to the inaugural address, we shall be in a better position to discern in it that distinctive quality here referred to as the Jeffersonian style.

Between Text and Context: A Note on Jeffersonian Style

In the spring of 1781 the Marquis de Chastellux journeyed from his encampment in Williamsburg up to the more serene environs of Monticello. After a few days with the newly retired (as Virginia gover- nor) Jefferson, the Marquis could only marvel at the range and depth of his new friend's learning: "Sometimes natural philosophy, at others politicks or the arts were the topicks of our conversation, for no object had escaped Mr. Jefferson," Chastellux later recalled, "[A]nd it seemed as if from his youth he had placed his mind, as he has done his house, on an elevated situation, from which he might contemplate the universe." That the mind and the house bore an analogous relationship to each other would in time become a frequent means to describe the peculiar style of Jefferson's thinking, where form and content combined to create a singular and lasting image of the man. It was a trait destined to command the admiration of his supporters and the scorn of his critics, but everyone who reflected on the matter recognized that in Jefferson the manner and the matter were one. As a recent scholar has put the case, Jefferson's "immense intellectual influence came through the cultivation of affinities within the American Enlightenment of the eighteenth century and the creation of symbols and images—Monticello comes to mind—that would reflect a secular, classical humanism in American thought."[26]

Among American presidents Lincoln alone rivals Jefferson as a prose stylist. But where Lincoln's formidable powers were trained almost exclusively on a single subject and to a single end, Jefferson's was applied over more than three decades of public life to an unmatched variety of problems and topics. From political tract to scientific treatise, from constitutions and charters, from correspondence to the inaugural address, he sought always to give to his ideas what John Adams memorably described as a "peculiar felicity of expression." Nearing our examination of the first inaugural address, accordingly, it will be worth our time to briefly dwell on the rhetorical quality that so distinguishes Jefferson's major writings. By way of a general strategy, we may recall the view previously advanced—that Jefferson offers in the address a stylized rendering of its own subject matter, a rhetorical instantiation of republican virtue, in short, a fusion of idiom and ideology. Students of Jefferson seldom fail to note how conspicuous was this feature: "Having something to say," Carl Becker noted, "he says it, with as much art as may be, yet not solely for the art's sake, aiming rather at the ease, the simplicity, and the genial urbanity of cultivated conversation. The grace and felicity of his style have a distinctively personal flavor, something

Jeffersonian in the implication of the idea, or in the beat and measure of his words."[27]

But what, more specifically, is this Jeffersonian "something"? Becker was an especially astute critic of Jefferson's rhetorical style, but like many others he turns in the end to vague or metaphorical descriptors to grasp the seemingly ineffable. Thus one reviewer notes in 1830 that the "style and character of Mr. Jefferson's writings resemble . . . those well drawn portraits, which regard and follow us with their eyes in whatever direction we move," while another assured readers of the *North American Review* that Jefferson was one of those rare geniuses who, "by combining literary and active pursuits, and exhibiting in both a first-rate talent, furnish in their works the most complete reflection that can possibly be given, of the finished man." Others have shown themselves less enthralled by Jefferson's characteristic style, especially as it worked to elevate his words above the mundane but pressing realities of political life. Joseph Ellis, perhaps the sharpest observer of Jefferson on this score, locates the Jeffersonian ethos within a larger and more complex matrix of executive, diplomatic, domestic, and republican styles evident throughout his public life. "The common ingredient in all these contexts," argues Ellis, "was Jefferson's urge to cloak his exercise of power from others and from himself."[28]

The point is at once simple and brilliant, for what Ellis discerns comes very close to identifying the persuasive achievement of the first inaugural address. As we have noted, the speech functions on a number of levels—as a partisan tract, as a political treatise—without announcing itself as either. The third level at which we are treating the address, as a rhetorical performance, allows us to see how such a cloaking operation takes place. That is to say, its rhetorical artistry consists in giving to republican principles their maximum aesthetic appeal; the result is a stylistically flawless rendering of arguments that from another perspective might well appear uncertain, exposed, or inconsistent. The inaugural address in this sense stands in an iconic relationship to the ideological energies swirling about and giving rise to it; put another way, the speech composes itself seamlessly as an unanswerable proclamation that this is what republicanism—true republicanism, American republicanism—looks and sounds like. The rough edges of politics are thereby filed smooth, power is honed and buffed to an exquisite finish, argument in the end burnished to the point where it disappears altogether.

It is worth reminding ourselves in this context that the inaugural address was the first major statement by Jefferson on political affairs that was not *overtly* oppositional (although, as we have seen, it was certainly partisan). *The Summary View,* the Declaration, the Kentucky Resolutions—all were played out in the crucible of intense political strife; now, in 1801, the speaker in effect proclaims the end of politics thus conceived and thus practiced. From here on out, politics was to be seen and heard on a different and truer register, played on a key set by the triumph of republican government and the new American nation. Jefferson aimed to place his country, like his mind and house, on what Chastellux rightly called an "elevated situation," an exalted and perfectly figured space where the prospects of nationhood could be glimpsed with breathtaking clarity. The first inaugural address allows us such a glimpse. Turning to it now, we will examine how it shapes our own view by (1) strategically constructing a particular image of the speaker; (2) by exemplifying norms of propriety; and (3) by embodying in its very language the virtues of republican simplicity.

A REPUBLICAN ETHOS

Neither critic nor champion could in 1801 dispute the republicanism of Thomas Jefferson. He brought with him to the podium a reputation for faith in its promises and commitment to its defense that few could match and none could supersede. At the same time, he must have known that reputation alone was insufficient to the task at hand; under the circumstances, Jefferson needed through the act of speech to craft and set on display his distinctive vision not only of what the nation had meant, but what it was to mean in the coming time. This much was to be demonstrated rather than assumed, created in and through the inaugural address as living testimony to the ideals he embraced. At stake in this process was the character of the speaker himself, and character, as Aristotle reminded readers of his *Rhetoric,* was "the controlling fac-

tor in persuasion." Here was no small challenge, if only because the inaugural ceremonies demanded of Jefferson talents for self-expression
nearly unprecedented in his public life. The speaker had spent a good
deal of his career in one role of opposition or another; he was by experience a writer of critical tracts, of declarations and resolutions against
constituted authority. Jefferson now occupied the highest office in the
land. How then to authorize *that* authority?[29]

Any response to the question would need to take into account a
rhetorical problem intrinsic to republicanism itself. Jefferson's position
demanded that he at once embody the principles of republican government, to give them eloquent voice and presence in speech, but not
so much as to eclipse by his person the democratic and equalitarian
ideals on which it was based and for which his office was but a con-
duit. Here was the very crux of all republican leadership. The problem
was not Jefferson's alone, but his response to it represents one of the
crowning rhetorical achievements of his life and that of his nation.

It is a matter of self and subject, and to better get at the means
through which he negotiates this delicate balance, we need first to ask
who Jefferson is in the speech. What work is this rhetorically crafted
person, this Jefferson-in-the-text, made to perform? How does the
image of the speaker, simultaneously projected from and supervising
the meaning in the text, organize and promote its values? One strategy
for addressing the question is to note the presence of first person pro-
nouns in the speech—the Jeffersonian "I"—and to observe how such
usage assists in forging the message as a whole. It is a modest measure,
to be sure, but an efficient and telling one, and it will reveal to us at
least one means through which Jefferson orchestrates a finely tuned
movement between one sense of authority (understood as a necessary
attribute of leadership) and another (understood as the province and
privilege of republicanism alone). Here the Jeffersonian style, so attuned
to the equipoise of opposites, may be seen in its most rhetorical
aspect.

The first person pronoun is used on twenty-one occasions in the
inaugural address. Of these, nearly half—nine—appear in the first of
its six paragraphs alone. At first glance, this repetition might seem to

violate the rhetorical convention of the *ingratio,* or the opening moments of a speech devoted to the effacement of the speaker in view of the greater needs of the moment and audience. On closer inspection, however, we see that in fact Jefferson stages these self-references in a highly strategic manner, at once drawing attention to his own role in bringing the day's events into being and establishing a becoming relationship to the complex of forces within which they are situated. This strategy is made especially evident when we note the verbs accompanying such usage: "I avail myself," "I approach it with those anxious and awful presentiments," "I contemplate these transcendent objects," "I shrink from the contemplation," "I shall find resources of wisdom," "I look with encouragement." Thus Jefferson's well-known modesty is at once underscored and put to work—not by coyly removing himself from the scene (his predecessor John Adams did not refer to himself until the fifth paragraph of his inaugural address), but by conspicuously subordinating himself to his audience, the nation, his office, and the Constitution. Like all good republicans, Jefferson understood that virtue was an essentially dramatic quality and that it, too, needed a stage on which it was to effect its ends.

Given the uncertainty and tensions of which this speech was an artifact, Jefferson's opening lines could not have been better conceived. Having triumphed over an "Anglican monarchical, and aristocratic party," having defeated the Anglo-leaning Adams and vanquished the aristocratic Hamilton, Jefferson needed now to occupy not a ground vacated by them but an entirely new, an entirely republican terrain. This he does in the inaugural address's brief introduction by subtly drawing attention to his presence in the near background of the drama; thus asserting by subordination, Jefferson in effect exemplifies the republican commitment to both the popular will and limited executive authority.[30]

The republican ethos made to superintend the work of paragraph one accordingly sets the terms for what follows. Here, in the long and complex second phase of the speech, Jefferson establishes an authorial perspective so poised as to reconcile and ultimately transcend the conflicts shaping—and misshaping—late eighteenth-century political culture. The authority to which Jefferson now lays claim and the credibility it confers has been secured by divesting himself of any desire for personal aggrandizement or self-interest. The stance is at once elevated and open, and from it the speaker can be seen seeing beyond the particulars of the moment, past the transient and surface elements to the heights and frontiers of the authentic nation. This act of conspicuous discernment is in turn made to illustrate precisely that quality of judgment necessary to republican leadership. It is altogether appropriate, then, that here Jefferson should exercise that judgment by asserting more positively his own active voice. Here the refrain involves not shrinking or contemplation or despair, but declarations of fact and faith: "I know, indeed, that some honest men fear that a republican government cannot be strong," "I believe this, on the contrary, the strongest Government on earth," "I believe it the only one where every man, at the call of the law, would fly to the standard of the law." By unavoidable implication, Jefferson's authority thus voiced is predicated on his capacity to command a perspective when others have been blinded by the winds of conflict; he must therefore reveal the delusion of others, correct their errors, remind them of the republican way.

Although clearly different in tone and function from the speech's opening lines, the second stands not in contrast but as an extension. If there is transformation here, it takes place by shifting to a different plane of symbolic action; that is, having expressed his reliance on the people for whatever authority he may exercise, Jefferson now assumes and applies that authority to realign a nation momentarily disordered by a malevolent few. They had done their work, but now, as Jefferson had noted to Joseph Priestly shortly after the speech, the "order and good sense displayed in this recovery from delusion, and in the momentous crisis which lately arose, really bespeak a strength of character in our nation which augurs well for the duration of our Republic." It is in part the task of this second paragraph to fuse the nation's "strength of character" to his own; hence Jefferson symbolically invites all true republicans onto the platform to see what he sees and to embrace each other in republican concord.[31]

In his politics as in his art, Jefferson reached for symmetry when he could find it. And when he did, he put that aesthetic principle to rhetorical ends, made it work in his writings and speeches to effect by words what he would create politically. Again, this constitutive interplay between idiom and ideology obliges us to look beyond broad thematic categories and attend, as we have, to textual particulars. With respect to the functions performed by the Jeffersonian "I," we can see in the speech's closing passages both this symmetry achieved formally and the rhetorical purposes to which that form is suited. The concluding two paragraphs recall the tone registered at the beginning and helps close, so to speak, the circle of the text's felicity. Some of this is owing to convention, prudence and assurances of good will being the better part of rhetorical wisdom. But we will have missed the more interesting entailments of this return by leaving it at that. As we saw in paragraphs one and two, we find here a similar effort to negotiate the speaker's self into an optimal relationship with those sources of power from which he must derive his own authority. Having introduced and ingratiated that self early in the speech and having asserted it in an image of enlightened reason in the middle, Jefferson now eases toward his exit by stepping backward while facing stage front:

"I repair, then, fellow-citizens, to the post you have assigned me"
"I have learnt to expect that it will rarely fall to the lot of imperfect man to retire from this station with the reputation and the favor which bring him into it"
"I ask so much confidence only as may give firmness and effect to the legal administration of your affairs"
"I shall often go wrong through defect of judgment"

Here is modesty befitting a republican leader. But lest we lose sight of Jefferson's own ends, we note, too, how careful he is not to let these constructions devolve into courtly obsequies. In truth there is nothing passive or even very deferential in these final lines, and we need not look far to see how the Jeffersonian "I" hints at a very near political future. Immediately after the steps taken above, that is, Jefferson takes several forward again by reminding his audience that those who would judge him critically may be viewed as "those whose positions will not command a view of the whole ground." Even as he takes his leave, then, Jefferson reinvokes the assertive phase in the body of the address and, promising never to err intentionally, begs his nation's "support against the errors of others, who may condemn what they would not if seen in all its parts." It is Jefferson and his followers, by fairly obvious juxtaposition, who in fact command such a view and see all the parts together—that is in no small measure what Jefferson took to be the essence of enlightened republican leadership. The final brief paragraph captures just this synthesis of personal authority and popular warrant so basic to Jefferson's unflagging optimism, and gives us reason to see why, in his words, "I advance with obedience to the work, ready to retire from it whenever you become sensible how much better choice it is in your power to make." That is old-fashioned political power wrapped in the plain but spotless glove of the republican style.

Republicanism was for Jefferson a revolutionary idea because it radically displaced power from its historical claimants and replaced it with popular sovereignty. That revolution—and truly it was—dramatically exposed the question of leadership divested of its monarchical trappings, parliamentary corruptions, and courtly intrigues. The question for the generation following independence was, What kind of authority, what kind of voice was appropriate to the task of leading a new nation "to destinies beyond the reach of mortal eye"? The answer, Jefferson understood, rested in the same place as the question—in the concept of republicanism itself, where the character of leadership was shaped always by the will of the people *and* a firm commitment to keep that people on its appointed errand. Thus the rhetorical power of the republican ethos but also its complexity: in Jefferson's address, it is a composite image of a leader whose authority comes from being authorized, an individual of unmistakable distinction who is also the symbolic embodiment of a revolutionary people and creed. And that, as Jefferson understood with equal force, requires style.

REPUBLICAN PROPRIETY

To lead as a republican, Jefferson demonstrated, was to exercise judgment of a kind and to give that judgment expression of a kind. It is this capacity for stylized discernment that accordingly distinguishes the first inaugural address, for in it can be seen the symbolic display of what a republican president ought to think and how he ought to say what he thinks. If a particular vision may be said to animate Jefferson's thought—a free people unfettered by artifice and arbitrary power— and if that thought was appropriately communicated with becoming simplicity—then we may ask where these two values intersect with greatest effect. Lest we fall err to separating the content and form of Jefferson's rhetorical art, we need to press on those dimensions of the text that seem to conjoin these two functions, and it is here, at the nodal point of his performance, that we discover where republican judgment (as manifested in the Jeffersonian ethos) and republican simplicity meet in the principle of *propriety*.

Surely no other statesman of his time was more attuned to questions of proportion than Thomas Jefferson. One need only survey at a glance the range of his activities to be struck by this lifelong preoccupation with measure, balance, decorum, fitness. Whether he was charting out a curriculum for aspirants to the bar, plotting revolution, practicing his violin, designing Monticello, making nails, reflecting on prosody, drafting constitutions, or planning administrative policy, Jefferson was consumed by the problem of what goes appropriately with what. This is above all a style of thought as much as it is thinking about style, and here we find a key for reading the inaugural address as a rhetorical performance. That it shaped his politics is evident throughout the several phases of his public life, especially as he considered what kinds of responses were appropriate to the assertion of power. Prior to the assent of his party to the executive office, Jefferson's writings on this score were primarily negative. He sought to explain in the Declaration the conditions under which it was fitting for a people, "disposed to suffer, while evils are sufferable," to declare themselves free and independent. So with Shay's rebellion, after which he urged leaders "not to be too severe upon their errors, but reclaim them by enlightening them," and argued that to "punish these errors too severely would be to suppress the only safeguard of the public liberty." Public condemnation of the democratic-republican societies Jefferson called an "extraordinary act of boldness," and the Alien and Sedition Acts "altogether void, and of no force."[32]

In each of these crises, government had been revealed as transgressing what was known to be the proper balance between instituted power and a republican citizenry. Because power, rightful power, could only rest with the people, any attempt to obviate it was on its face suspect, no more clearly than when governments sought to squelch the popular uprising inevitable in a republican country. This was why, as Jefferson famously wrote to Abigail Adams, "I like a little rebellion now and then, it is like a storm in the Atmosphere," and why "this truth should render honest republican governors so mild in their punishment of rebellions, as not to discourage them too much." Governments failing to react mildly lacked a sense of proportion, that principle of propriety, so essential to the faith. At best they assented to the tenets of republicanism, but did not understand what forms of action such conviction entailed. To grasp that distinction was, by contrast, to grasp both essence and practice; it meant that the assertion of principle necessarily implied a course of behavior through which that principle was to be realized to full advantage. Here then is the function of propriety as a marker of political style: the capacity to arrange all factors in a situation so as to create and sustain the conditions for principled action. It is characterized specifically by a dialectic of assertion and restraint, of saying what must be said but no more and no less.[33]

Jefferson's inaugural address allows us to see this sense of propriety at work in less abstract terms. Here he undertakes in two phases to provide a model of reasoning proportionate to the circumstances at hand: in the first, he explicitly indicates which modes of action are attendant to the principles declared; in the second, he defers to the wisdom of the people by conspicuously leaving such prescriptions unstated. But whether stated or implied, the direction of Jefferson's argument remains the same: in all cases of uncertainty, novelty, or crisis, the appropriate response for a republican people is to return to the essential principles of the American experiment. His speech operates accordingly to state those essential principles with the authority granted his person and office, to do so with the utmost simplicity, and to remind his auditors of how they are to compose themselves in view of those principles.

Propriety, like simplicity, is a virtue requiring no little art. It is, for one thing, called for precisely when exigencies are most unsettling and disorganized. Rhetorically speaking, propriety is made more complex because it seems to work best when noticed least. Thus Aristotle observes that when propriety is at stake, the "author should compose without being noticed and should seem to speak not artificially but naturally," for "if one composes well, there will be an unfamiliar quality and it escapes notice and will be clear." This, we may suppose, serves better than most to explain Jefferson's "peculiar felicity of expression." In the specific context of his inaugural address, it characterizes an unfolding process through which principles and the actions they entail are organized with such elegant clarity as to elide their artful management. Bending to the prose more closely, however, we may see that art as clearly as the politics it promotes. In the first phase of this process, Jefferson establishes a recurrent pattern of signification, initially by pointing to a state of instability, then to a principle essential to republican government, and finally to modes of action appropriate to the realization of that principle. The effect, again, is to set on display an example of propriety as both a political and rhetorical virtue.[34]

What, in short, is the proper or fitting response to "the contest of opinion" though which Americans had recently passed? True, so bumptious had been that experience that "strangers" became alarmed and doubted the prospects of republicanism altogether. To this question Jefferson posits the answer by reference to the Constitution and the principle of rule by law. Consequently, he confidently predicts, all will now "arrange themselves" under that rule, will "unite in common efforts for the common good," and "bear in mind" the balance between majority will and minority rights essential to republican government. A similar ordering is evident in Jefferson's portrayal of the international and domestic upheavals shaping the recent decade, when "religious intolerance," "bitter and bloody persecutions," "the throes and convulsions of the ancient world," "the agonizing spasms of infuriated man," and the "agitation of the billows" threatened domestic concord. In the face of these formidable elements, Jefferson again summons the principle of republican government, "the world's best hope." And, again, he underscores what kind of action is fitting to those living within its auspices: they will "fly to the standard of the law," they will "meet invasions of the public" as their own concerns, they will trust themselves with government by themselves. It is, moreover, perfectly consistent with Jefferson's republican propriety that he not elaborate upon nor vilify those who would resist the tide of such government: hence the much-observed tone of conciliation and temperance that shades the address. To do otherwise would on its own terms violate the standards of restraint appropriate to the assertion of republican principle.

Knowing what *not* to say is as key to the exercise of republican propriety as what *must* be said. This much we have seen in the breach with regard to Federalist reactions of the past decade. But the rule suggests something more than tactical prudence, a desire to seem "mild" by contrast to the excesses of one's opponents. Some of this is at work, of course, but the more general assumption has to do with the nature of republican thought itself. In Jefferson's view, the people were naturally inclined to act for the good of themselves and their fellow citizens; to activate this civic virtue, they needed only to see the principle to act on its behalf. In other words, there was no need for dwelling on differences because the audience was presumptively agreed upon the constants of their collective identity. Indeed, the sheer act of not saying something, of relying on the implied, the axiomatic, and the silently acknowledged underscores the common sense of the matter being expressed. Having recalled and reorganized the complex of persons, events, and values to their rightful and fitting relationship, Jefferson can now proceed in the address in the most efficient, the most appropriate manner—that is, by simply stating the principles sure to guide his government. In this way, he signals to his audience a complete trust in their capacity to grasp the essence of his (hence their own) thought and to arrange themselves accordingly. Paragraphs three and four thus represent a virtual compendium of republican principles, compressed, as Jefferson says, "within the narrowest compass they will bear." Such narrow compass—no qualifications, "limitations," or hedging—is granted because the source, direction, and authority of these principles are already acknowledged by all true republicans. In this case, ideology is made to rest easily within an idiom ideally suited to the needs of the speaker, the audience, and the occasion. Like vessels journeying to sacred shores, each element in Jefferson's universe is bound by common laws, each distinctive in its own right, equidistant to the other and moving in paths brightened by enlightened humanity. From this perspective, that is fitting which conduces to the forward motion of the republican "argosie"; that which intervenes or retards this motion could only be the grossest violation of natural law.

REPUBLICANISM AND THE VIRTUES OF SIMPLICITY

On the eve of revolution Thomas Paine promised readers of his wildly popular pamphlet "nothing more than simple facts, plain arguments, and common sense." The author delivered on that promise to unprecedented effect, and in the process helped enshrine a key principle of republican letters: "the more simple anything is," Paine averred, "the less liable it is to be disordered." Unlike the tortured and artificially complex style typical of aristocratic prose, republican writing was henceforth to express itself in language that was clear, natural, and unadorned by the linguistic pretensions of his British opponents. How one argued, with what style and tone, was thus not incidental but essential to the politics being argued. As John Quincy Adams later explained, "Our institutions . . . are republican," then "Persuasion, or the influence of reason and feeling, is the great if not the only instrument, whose operation can affect the acts of all our corporate bodies." And if the art of persuasion was to prove up to such a task, it must therefore give to republican government its optimal mode of expression, must express itself in a style that was, as Paine wrote, "simple," "plain," and "common."[35]

No other figure in the early republic better exemplified this style—at once a political and rhetorical virtue—than Thomas Jefferson. His prose was widely acknowledged, as we have seen, for its "felicity of expression," not alone in the Declaration but in the *Summary View,* the *Notes on the State of Virginia,* even in the more strident Kentucky Reso-

lutions. Like comedy, however, simplicity of style is a deceptively difficult achievement, the effect of great discipline and even greater art. He
who would seek it, Cicero noted in *De oratore*, "must clothe his thoughts
in such a manner as to comprise them in a flow of numbers, at con-
fined to measure, yet free from restraint; for, after restricting it to proper
modulation and structure, he gives it an ease and freedom by a variety
in the flow, so that the words are neither bound by strict laws, as those
of verse, nor yet have such a degree of liberty as to wander without
control." Jefferson, who knew his Cicero well, would have found on his
shelves other volumes stressing much the same point; thus Hugh Blair's
standard *Lectures on Rhetoric and Belles Lettres* insisted that perspicuity "is the fundamental quality of style, a quality so essential in every
kind of writing, that for the want of it, nothing can atone. Without this,"
Blair concluded, "the richest ornaments of style only glimmer through
the dark; and puzzle, instead of pleasing the reader."[36]

The form and content of the first inaugural address cannot, therefore, be put asunder; to grasp its politics is to grasp the style with which
it is given expression. There are a variety of ways in which this interplay may be observed, but perhaps one approach will suffice in making the point. As a model of republican simplicity, the speech displays
three prominent metaphors; while unobtrusive, these tropes shape and
direct the ideological force of the message in important ways. In the
image of the *vessel,* the *circle,* and the *road,* Jefferson renders his ideas
to striking effect; he thus gives us reason to briefly identify and trace
out the entailments of each as evidence of the speaker's rhetorical art.

Several days after delivering his inaugural address, Jefferson assured
John Dickinson that "the storm though which we have passed, has been
tremendous indeed. The tough sides of our Argosie have been thoroughly tried. Her strength has stood the waves into which she was
steered, with a view to sink her." Optimistic as always, Jefferson nevertheless was certain that now "We shall put her on her republican tack,
and she will now show by the beauty of her motion the skill of her
builders."[37] The vessel of state was of course a prominent image in eighteenth-century letters, and Jefferson was fond of it, capturing as it did
so well the otherwise complex associations of adventure and uncertainty

that was the republican experiment. It was altogether appropriate, therefore, that he should employ the metaphor early in the inaugural address: "To you, then, gentlemen, who are charged with the sovereign functions of legislation, and to those associated with you, I look with encouragement for that guidance and support which may enable us to steer with safety the vessel in which we are all embarked amidst the conflicting elements of a troubled world."

Jefferson, who had little experience with nautical life beyond transport across the Atlantic, nevertheless grasped fully the range and resonance of the image. Here, as later with reference to federal government as "the sheet anchor of our peace at home and safety abroad," the speaker captures in very few words a rich array of meanings. Chief among these is the relationship struck between peril and collective effort; that is, we see in these lines on the one hand the sense of danger and conflict confronting the ship of state, and on the other the prospects for safe passage should captain and crew work harmoniously together. All the opportunities, the riches and success of republican government, Jefferson implies, lay just ahead on the nation's rapidly approaching horizon; without a shared sense of purpose and mutual aid, however, that future must remain clouded and ominous. Given the tempests of the past decade, this image, so simple and yet so resonant, is ideally suited to the speaker's rhetorical purposes.

In the vessel Jefferson found a figure of speech denoting containment as well as expanse, community as well as direction and progress. In the image of the circle, he discovers a means to give this set of dynamics a more abstract but equally forceful expression. Jefferson was, as Ellis has abundantly demonstrated, possessed of a mind given to abstractions of all kinds—and not always to happy effect. Certainly he tended to lift from the disorder and debris of experience structures of meaning that could comprehend ever-higher orders of significance; to his critics, this was evidence of a visionary and impractical cast of mind; to his supporters, it was the very stuff of genius. In any case, the figure of the circle gave to Jefferson an equally simple but powerful means to say a great deal in few words: "[W]hat more is necessary to make us a happy and a prosperous people? Still one thing more, fellow-citizens;

a wise and frugal Government, which shall restrain men from injuring one another, shall leave them otherwise free to regulate their own pursuits of industry and improvement, and shall not take from the mouth of labor the bread it has earned. This is the sum of good government, and this is necessary to close the circle of our felicities." As with the vessel metaphor, in the circle we find a wealth of entailments that belies the simplicity of the figure itself. In general we may note that it is at once abstract but universally recognizable; visual but not beholden to contingent experience; an ideal form and a concrete image. More specifically, we see how it functions in the preceding passage to shape complex matter into elegant form. Its usage here serves, like that of the vessel, a double function: it imposes a symmetrical order onto the flux of experience, *and* it does so without appearing to restrain the expansive energies that constitute the life of the nation.

It is worth noting in this regard that the paragraph closed by the "circle of our felicities" is devoted to an aggregation of claims and principles conspicuous for their expansive and transformative tendencies. Jefferson thus closes that circle not as a way of circumscribing his "empire of liberty," but by identifying the form of government necessary for its extension. Hence republicanism gets envisioned as an expanding circle, perfectly ordered, self-evident in its truth, clearly demarcated from what it is not but infinitely capable of containing that which belongs rightfully to it. And it is, of course, an image of politics that will motivate some of the best and worst ambitions of America for centuries to come; for the moment, however, it was to prove as useful, as stylistically and ideologically fitting an image as might be imagined.

The nautical and geometric tropes at work in this speech give to its message both shape and direction. As a result, they dramatize in their very efficiency of statement what Jefferson envisions of republican government: principles activated by common purpose and formed by historical experience and future aspirations. In their different significations, the vessel and the circle represent variations on this theme of the republican mission. That mission, at once backward- and forward-looking, is further emplotted into the speech through the metaphor of the journey. Again, this is scarcely unique to Jefferson—in fact it is perhaps the single most enduring figure in American rhetorical culture. From the days of the puritans until this day, the concept of America's errand undergirds virtually every major social, religious, and political transformation to which this nation has been subject. Jefferson's appeal to it would then have been wholly recognizable to his audience, and he could trust his readers and listeners to take from his words precisely what he meant:

> These principles form the bright constellation which has gone before us and guided our steps through an age of revolution and reformation. The wisdom of our sages and blood of our heroes have been devoted to their attainment. They should be the creed of our political faith, the text of civic instruction, the touchstone by which to try the services of those we trust; and should we wander from them in moments of error or of alarm, let us hasten to retrace our steps and to regain the road which alone leads to peace, liberty, and safety.

Here as in the previous two instances, the image of the path or road works on several levels to secure the speaker's intentions. We note, for example, how it reproduces on land what Jefferson earlier alluded to in terms of the sea: that all are gathered as on a journey; that while hazardous, hope is to be found in the wisdom of the people and the principles to which all pay obeisance; and that, ultimately, it is a journey toward a greater world. It is especially important in this context to appreciate Jefferson's stress on what was required to keep Americans on this road—or, having fallen off it, what was to return them again.

The principles enunciated in paragraphs two and three are to be read as a "bright constellation," a "creed of our political faith," a "text of civic instruction," a "touchstone." In short, the prospects of republican government are enlightened as the people are enlightened, taught, that is, to see in the rule of law and the values upon which they rest a template for civic action. A secular analogue to the Mosaic tradition, this image of a people guided by the laws to its destined fulfillment takes on poignant dimensions: who more than Americans have been so confident that their journey could in fact be realized? And who among Americans was at once more certain, more anxious, that the new nation "regain the road which alone leads to peace, liberty, and safety" than Thomas Jefferson?

Conclusion

To interpret the inaugural address as a rhetorical performance is to seek after its craft, the tactical and artistic management of language to secure the conviction of its auditors. It is not for that reason to isolate the text from its other tasks; as we have seen in previous chapters, Jefferson can be read with equal profit as giving expression to partisan principles and to a certain conception of nationhood. The rhetorical work of the text is to consolidate and give force to those principles, even as it exemplifies them through the strategic choice of words, images, and appeals. I have sought in this chapter to demonstrate the nuances of Jefferson's art of effective expression; to that end, we have examined the text with reference to the traditions of which he availed himself, including sermons, civic commemorations, and political debate. The task has been made more challenging by acknowledging that Jefferson's own relation to the rhetorical arts generally was complex, and that he cannot be considered in any normal sense an orator as such. But we have seen that this need not limit access to the ambitions at work behind the speech nor its exquisite rendering of principle. If anything, close attention to the internal dynamics and external energies circulating through it can only confirm the judgment of posterity—that here we have an exemplar of its kind.

Jefferson's rhetorical art has not always and everywhere been met with unalloyed enthusiasm. Critics in his own time took him to task for stylistic pretension and partisan stealth, for speaking in airy abstractions and self-serving platitudes. Charles Francis Adams later could charge that Jefferson "has left hanging over a part of his public life a vapor of duplicity, or, to say the least, of indirection, the presence of which is generally felt more than it is seen." More damningly, Carl Becker granted Jefferson's "felicity of expression," but noted, too, that such felicity "gives one at times a certain feeling of insecurity, as of resting one's weight on something fragile. Jefferson's placidity," Becker concluded, "the complacent optimism of his sentiments and ideas, carry him at times perilously near the fatuous. One would like more evidence that the iron had some time or other entered his soul, more evidence of having profoundly reflected on the enigma of existence, of having more deeply felt its tragic import, of having won his convictions and his optimisms and his felicities at the expense of some travail of the spirit." Becker's insight is keen: in his rhetorical craft as in his thought, Jefferson could appear almost too eloquent, as if in the finely crafted sentiment he could make the world over again, in his image, to his own satisfaction, heedless of others.[38]

Perhaps. Without dismissing such suspicions, it may be worth reflecting as well on what it is that animates both the performance and our abiding interest in it. To ask that question is to ask after the man himself and, ultimately, the cultural forces that sustain the speech on the winds of history. That much is beyond the scope of this project, but we have at least the beginnings of an answer here. The "faculty of observing in any given case the available means of persuasion" to which Aristotle alluded was Jefferson's own. With it, he discerned like no one else what was lasting in the American soul; here was the source and object of his words, and with them he eloquently summoned his fellow republicans to a better version of themselves.

Epilogue

Thomas Jefferson professed to be above party; claimed no exalted status as a political theorist; declined the orator's laurel. I have attempted in these chapters to suggest that in fact Jefferson was not above party, that he was a political thinker of genuine stature, and that he was, if not an orator, then certainly a master of giving to principle the force of artistic expression. None of this will perhaps come as a surprise to specialists in Jefferson and his time, and in truth I have sought less to establish a novel thesis than to illuminate the inaugural address through a series of close readings. The result, I hope, is to have brought that text into clearer focus, to see it now as intersected by a variety of traditions, motives, and effects. The operative premise in this analysis—that the speech yields productively to several lines of inquiry—has led us to consider it as simultaneously partisan, theoretical, and rhetorical. Rather than impose these categories from above or as mutually exclusive, I have tried to indicate how they are generated from the text itself and cohere into an organically unified statement on the prospects of republican government.

As a partisan tract, Jefferson's address was designed to announce and effect the triumph of the republican party at a moment of crisis in the nation's young life. The speaker may have protested otherwise; he may have eschewed party in principle; he may have convinced himself that there was no authentic distinction between republicanism and Republicanism. But others knew better, including his many supporters. "The voice of a majority of the people has declared itself in favor, not only of particular men, but of particular measures," crowed the *National Intelligencer*. "The contest, which has just passed, was a contest of principle. A decision has been made; and power [has] been entrusted to those who have been considered as attached to certain principles, and to measures calculated to give them effect." For a short time, at least, Jefferson may well have thought the vindication complete: the party and the nation could seem, from a certain angle, as one. History was to prove otherwise soon enough. The inaugural address, in any case, may now be seen as classically Jeffersonian in its happy appeal to both principle and expedience, its elegant dismissal of opposition, the exquisite harmony with which it reorders a troubled world.[1]

Viewed from a different perspective, the inaugural address stands as a succinct expression of Jefferson's political thought generally and his nationalism in particular. At the foundations of this thought was a set of convictions about human nature as inherently social and sympathetic. Not that people inevitably acted according to this potential; the long train of abuses meted out by history's tyrants provided plenty of evidence to the contrary. It was rather the task of government to so organize and secure the affections of society as to realize in polity what nature gave in trust. Republican government, because it rested on no other authority than the people themselves, was the only form suited to such ends. In effect, it was but the political expression of human nature; thus virtue, the willing capacity to subordinate private interest to the public and collective good, found its appropriate expression in a government of the people. At the other corner of this foundation rested the principle of liberty, seen not in competition with but as a complement to republican virtue. Liberty meant for Jefferson the freedom to realize as fully as possible one's destiny as a human and, by extension, as humans in concert with one another. Jefferson's nationalism—his view of what America was and could be, his foreign and domestic ambitions—thus represents his commitment both to American self-determination and to the spread of republican government throughout the world.

As a rhetorical performance, finally, the inaugural address stages the pageant of America at the outset of a new century. The chief herald of the "republican millennium," Jefferson was clearly no orator along the lines of Henry before him nor Webster after. His voice was to be heard on a different register: restrained, decorous, with a simplicity becoming the republican leader of a democratizing society. His performance of March 4, 1801, was his alone—it is impossible to imagine anyone else composing it—but it worked as it did because it drew from traditions of thought and speech, authorized itself by appeal to common truths and widely shared aspirations. Its eloquence rested in saying the most in the fewest words, in compressing into itself no less than a party manifesto, a theory of nationhood, and a model of how republican language ought to look and sound. In the traditions of American presidential rhetoric, Lincoln alone could lay claim to an equivalent capacity for crafting the language through which a nation was to speak itself.

There is, of course, much that remains to be discussed and discovered. Such preoccupation with a single text inevitably selects out a great deal of importance, including many issues at the forefront of Jefferson studies today. Above all, I have not attended in any systematic manner to what Jefferson did *not* say, to the many ellipses, implications, and silences that mark even this prolific public figure. By way of modest compensation, I have tried to recall something of the man's complexity by refusing to cut him out of cardboard, to acknowledge his limitations as well as his achievements and balance praise with blame. In this I have been assisted by a long and vociferous train of critics and champions, those innumerable Americans who have from the beginning found it impossible to keep quiet about the reserved Virginian.

The aim throughout has been to lean close to Jefferson, to hear and see him speak as clearly as possible, to feel the proximity of his words even as we reflect from afar. If there is merit in this, it rests in having observed not only the act of speech but why that act continues to assert itself on our collective conscious. For the ideals and aspirations found in the inaugural address still resonate, and that is as true as it is wondrous. Jefferson has served to leverage competing accounts of American nationhood well before his providential death on July 4 of 1826; through the Jacksonian years, the Civil War and Reconstruction, the Progressive era and New Deal, the Cold War and its unknown aftermath. Many of the principles we associate with Jefferson's legacy have no doubt lost their cultural purchase; still, as one historian has written, "he may yet go on vindicating his power in the national life as the heroic voice of imperishable freedoms. It is this Jefferson," concludes Merrill Peterson, "who stands at the radiant center of his own history, and who makes for the present a symbol that unites the nation's birth with its inexorable ideal."[2] Peterson's words, written almost a half-century ago, remain as true of Jefferson today as then. And that is a fact owing in no small way to the achievement of his first inaugural address.

Notes

Introduction

1. Henry Adams, *History of the United States of America*, 2:185, 196.
2. As based on the text in Merrill Peterson, ed. *Thomas Jefferson: Writings*, 492–96. For purposes of convenience to the reader, all further citations of the inaugural address are to this edition; *Independent Chronicle*, March 3, 1801, 2; Du Pont de Nemour to Thomas Jefferson, in Dumas Malone, ed., *Correspondence Between Thomas Jefferson and Pierre Samuel Du Pont Nemour, 1798–1817*, trans. Linwood Lehman, 30; Thomas Jefferson to James Monroe, quoted in George Tucker, *The Life of Thomas Jefferson*, 1:xi.
3. Tucker, *Life of Thomas Jefferson*, 2:85; Henry Randall, *The Life of Thomas Jefferson*, 633.
4. Tom Watson, *The Life and Times of Thomas Jefferson*, 398; Woodrow Wilson, quoted in "Jefferson-Wilson: A Record and a Forecast," *North American Review* 197 (1913): 291; Fawn M. Brodie, *Thomas Jefferson: An Intimate History*, 336; Peter S. Onuf, *Jefferson's Empire: The Language of American Nationhood*, 106.
5. For recent discussions of the Sally Hemings controversy, see Jan Ellen Lewis and Peter S. Onuf, eds., *Sally Hemings and Thomas Jefferson: History, Memory, and Civic Culture*; and Annette Gordon-Reed, *Thomas Jefferson and Sally Hemings: An American Controversy*; on the historical career of Jefferson's relationship to slavery, see especially Merrill Peterson, *The Jefferson Image in the American Mind*; and, more recently, Scot A. French and Edward L. Ayers, "The Strange Career of Thomas Jefferson: Race and Slavery in American Memory, 1943–1993" in Peter S. Onuf, ed., *Jeffersonian Legacies*, 418–56.
6. Jay Fliegelman, *Declaring Independence: Jefferson, Natural Language, and the*

Culture of Performance; Sandra M. Gustafson, *Eloquence is Power: Oratory and Performance in Early America;* and Thomas Gustafson, *Representative Words: Politics, Literature, and the American Language, 1776–1865;* Christopher Looby, *Voicing America: Language, Literary Form, and the Origins of the United States;* and Michael Warner, *The Letters of the Republic: Publication and the Public Sphere in Eighteenth-Century America.* Aristotle, in George A. Kennedy, *Aristotle on Rhetoric: A Theory of Civic Discourse,* 36.

7. Thomas Jefferson to Francis Hopkinson, March 13, 1789, in *Writings,* 940–41.

8. Charles Francis Adams, *The Works of John Adams,* 1:616.

9. John Adams, "Autobiography," in ibid., 2:511.

Chapter 1. "Brethren of the Same Principle": The First Inaugural Address and the Language of Party

1. John Quincy Adams to Rufus King, Oct. 13, 1801, in Worthington C. Ford, ed., *Writings of John Quincy Adams,* 3:1; *Aurora,* March 6, 1801, 2.

2. John R. Howe, "Republican Thought and the Political Violence of the 1790s," *American Quarterly* 19 (1967), 148; Thomas Jefferson, quoted in ibid., 148.

3. *New England Palladium,* March 31, 1801, 1.

4. *Gazette of the United States,* March 5, 1801, 2; *Salem Impartial Register,* March 16, 1801, 3.

5. Woodrow Wilson, quoted in "Jefferson-Wilson: A Record and a Forecast," 291; *Gazette of the United States,* March 12, 1801, 3; *Salem Impartial Register,* March 19, 1801, 2; *Aurora,* March 18, 1801, 2.

6. Theodore Dwight, *The Character of Thomas Jefferson,* 338; Alexander Hamilton, "An Address to the Electors of the State of New-York," in *The Papers of Alexander Hamilton,* ed. Harold C. Syrett, 25:365; "lullaby" quoted in Claude G. Bowers, *Jefferson in Power: The Death Struggle of the Federalists,* 54–55; *Gazette of the United States,* April 15, 1801, 2.

7. Tucker, *Life of Thomas Jefferson,* 2:86–87.

8. Merrill Peterson, *Thomas Jefferson and the New Nation: A Biography,* 656; Joseph Ellis, *American Sphinx: The Character of Thomas Jefferson,* 216.

9. Stanley Elkins and Eric McKitrick, *The Age of Federalism,* 196–97.

10. Edmund Burke, in *The Correspondence of Edmund Burke,* ed. Lucy Sutherland, 2:101; *Thoughts on the Cause of the Present Discontents,* vol. 1, *The Works of Edmund Burke,* 530, 526; see also Stephen H. Browne, "Edmund Burke's Discontents and the Interpretation of Political Culture," *Quarterly Journal of Speech* 77 (1991): 53–66.

11. Gordon S. Wood, *The Creation of the American Republic, 1776–1787,* 58.

12. Richard Hofstadter, *The Idea of a Party System: The Rise of Legitimate Opposition in the United States, 1780–1840,* 12; John Trenchard, quoted in ibid., 15.

13. Thomas Gordon and John Trenchard, *Cato's Letters,* 265.

14. Henry St. John Viscount Bolingbroke, quoted in Hofstadter, *Party System,* 21.

15. Ibid., 19; Bolingbroke, "A Dissertation on Parties," in *Bolingbroke's Political Writings,* ed. Bernard Cottret, 33.

16. David Hume, "Of Parties in General," in *David Hume's Political Essays,* ed. Charles W. Hendel, 77–78.

17. Hofstadter, *Party System,* 2; Wood, *Creation of the American Republic,* 59.

18. George Washington, Farewell Address, in *American Rhetorical Discourse,* ed. Ronald F. Reid, 220; Howe, "Republican Thought," 149.

19. Washington, Farewell, 215.

20. Ibid., 216, 217.

21. Hofstadter, *Party System,* 99.

22. Joyce Appleby, *Capitalism and a New Social Order: The Republican Vision of the 1790s,* 4; Thomas Jefferson to Elbridge Gerry, Jan. 26, 1799, in *Writings,* 1055; Lance Banning, *The Jeffersonian Persuasion: Evolution of a Party Ideology,* 162.

23. James Rogers Sharp, *American Politics in the Early Republic: The New Nation in Crisis,* 10; David N. Mayer, *The Constitutional Thought of Thomas Jefferson,* 114.

24. Thomas Jefferson to John Taylor, June 4, 1798, in *Writings,* 1050; Jefferson to James Madison, March 15, 1789, in *Writings,* 994–95.

25. Appleby, *Capitalism,* 6; Thomas Jefferson to William Branch Giles, quoted in William Nisbet Chambers, *Political Parties in the New Nation: The American Experience, 1776–1809,* 93.

26. Thomas Jefferson to John Taylor, June 4, 1798, in *Writings,* 1050; Jefferson to Gerry, Jan. 26, 1799, in *Writings,* 1058.

27. *National Intelligencer,* March 6, 1801, 3; *Pittsburgh Gazette,* March 20, 1801, 3; *National Intelligencer,* March 9, 1801, 3.

28. Joseph Hale to Rufus King, Aug. 6, 1801, in *The Life and Correspondence of Rufus King,* ed. Charles R. King, 495; Robert Goodloe Harper, *Connecticut Courant,* March 6, 1801, 1; Pierre Samuel de Nemour to Thomas Jefferson, in *Correspondence Between Thomas Jefferson and Pierre Samuel Du Pont Nemour,* 36.

29. Thomas Jefferson to John Dickinson, March 6, 1801, in *Writings,* 1084; Jefferson to Monroe, March 7, 1801, quoted in Tucker, *Life of Thomas Jefferson,* 2:91.

30. Thomas Jefferson to Gideon Granger, Aug. 13, 1800, in *Writings,* 1079–80; Sharp, *American Politics,* 12–13.

31. Hofstadter, *Party System,* 151.

32. *Gazette of the United States,* April 11, 1801, 3.

33. Stephen Lucas, "Justifying America: The Declaration of Independence as a Rhetorical Document," in *American Rhetoric: Contexts and Criticism,* ed., Thomas W. Benson, 76.

34. Jefferson to Dickinson, March 6, 1801, in *Writings,* 1084.

35. Thomas Jefferson to Joseph Priestly, March 21, 1801, in ibid., 1086.

36. Jefferson to Gerry, Jan. 26, 1799, in ibid., 1057; Thomas Jefferson to Benjamin Rush, Sept. 23, 1800, in ibid., 1082.

37. Griswold quoted in Noble E. Cunningham, Jr., *The Jeffersonian Republicans in Power: Party Operations, 1801–1809,* 10; Onuf, *Jefferson's Empire,* 15.

38. Ellis, *American Sphinx,* 218–19.

39. Onuf, *Jefferson's Empire,* 15, 14.

40. Jefferson to Hopkinson, March 13, 1789, in *Writings,* 941.

41. Banning, *Jeffersonian Persuasion,* 177.

Chapter 2. *"The Strongest Government on Earth": The First Inaugural Address as Political Theory*

1. Joseph Ellis, *Founding Brothers: The Revolutionary Generation.*

2. Peterson, *New Nation,* 28–29.

3. John Marshall, quoted in Dumas Malone, *Jefferson the President: First Term,*

1801–1805, 22; Timothy Pinckney, quoted in ibid., 177; John Adams, quoted in ibid., 322; John Beckley, quoted in ibid., 484.

4. Garrett Ward Sheldon, *The Political Philosophy of Thomas Jefferson*, 3; Joyce Appleby, *Capitalism;* Morton White, *The Philosophy of the American Revolution;* Michael P. Zuckert, "Response," in *Thomas Jefferson and the Politics of Nature*, ed. Thomas S. Engeman, 192.

5. J. R. Pole, "Jefferson and the Pursuit of Equality," in *Reason and Republicanism: Thomas Jefferson's Legacy of Liberty*, eds., Gary L. McDowell and Sharon L. Noble, 219.

6. Robert Booth Fowler, "Mythologies of a Founder," in Engeman, *Politics of Nature*, 623–24; Ellis, *Founding Brothers*, 231.

7. Daniel J. Boorstin, *The Lost World of Thomas Jefferson*, 8; Dumas Malone, *Jefferson the Virginian*, xv; Colin Bonwick, "Jefferson as Nationalist," in McDowell and Noble, *Reason and Republicanism*, 152.

8. Thomas Jefferson to William Green Munford, June 18, 1799, in *Writings*, 1064; Francis Hutchinson, quoted in Jean M. Yarbrough, "The Moral Sense, Character Formation, and Virtue," in McDowell and Noble, *Reason and Republicanism*, 274.

9. Thomas Jefferson to Peter Carr, Aug. 10, 1797, in *Writings*, 901; Thomas Jefferson to Thomas Law, June 13, 1814, in *Writings*, 1337–38; Gary Wills, *Inventing America: Jefferson's Declaration of Independence* offers a provocative though flawed interpretation of Jefferson's relationship to the Scottish philosophy.

10. Gordon Wood, "The Trials and Tribulations of Thomas Jefferson, in Onuf, *Jeffersonian Legacies*, 405–406; Yarbrough, "Moral Sense," 271–303.

11. Benjamin Franklin, quoted in H. Trevor Colbourn, *The Lamp of Experience: Whig History and the Intellectual Origins of the American Revolution*, 131; Wood, *Creation*, 68; Banning, *Jeffersonian Persuasion*, 46.

12. Joyce Appleby, *Liberalism and Republicanism in the Historical Imagination*, 185.

13. Sheldon, *Political Philosophy*, 60; Appleby, *Liberalism*, 299.

14. Baron de Montesquieu, quoted in Sheldon, *Political Philosophy*, 64.

15. Jefferson to Priestly, March 21, 1801, in *Writings*, 1085.

16. Jefferson to Law, June 13, 1814, in ibid., 1338.

17. Ibid.

18. Thomas Jefferson, Notes on the State of Virginia, in ibid., 290.

19. Jefferson to Law, June 13, 1814, in ibid., 1336–37.

20. John Hurt, quoted in Wood, *Creation*, 69.

21. Thomas Jefferson, A Summary View of the Rights of British Americans, in *Writings*, 122; Thomas Jefferson to Roger C. Weightman, June 24, 1826, in ibid., 1517.

22. Benjamin Church, quoted in Wood, *Creation*, 24; Enos Hitchcock, "An Oration in Commemoration of the Independence of the United States of America," in *Political Sermons of the Founding Era, 1730–1815*, ed. Ellis Sandoz, 1177.

23. Following Banning, *Jeffersonian Persuasion*; Peter Thacher, "A Sermon Preached Before the Artillery Company," in Sandoz, *Political Sermons*, 1142–43.

24. Jefferson to Rush, Sept. 23, 1800, in *Writings*, 1082; Jefferson, Draft of the Kentucky Resolutions, in *Writings*, 455.

25. Appleby, *Capitalism*, 16–23; Thomas Jefferson, Bill for Establishing Religious Freedom, in *Writings*, 346; Jefferson to Munford, June 18, 1799, in *Writings*, 1065.

26. Peterson, *New Nation*, 657.

27. Bernard Bailyn, *The Ideological Origins of the American Revolution*, 56.

28. James H. Read, *Power Versus Liberty: Madison, Hamilton, Wilson, and Jefferson*, 120.

29. John Locke, quoted in Sheldon, *Political Philosophy*, 10–11.

30. Jefferson to Gerry, Jan. 26, 1799, in *Writings*, 1056; Thomas Jefferson to Philip Mazzei, April 24, 1796, in *Writings*, 1037.

31. Thomas Jefferson to Madame d'Enville, April 2, 1790, in *Writings*, 965.

32. Tench Coxe, *A View of the United States of America* (Philadelphia, 1795), 428; Thomas Jefferson to James Madison, June 9, 1793, in *Writings*, 1011.

33. George Berkeley, quoted in Kenneth Silverman, *A Cultural History of the American Revolution*, xiv.

34. Julian Boyd, "Thomas Jefferson's 'Empire of Liberty,'" in Merrill D. Peterson, *Thomas Jefferson: A Profile*, 188; Onuf, *Jefferson's Empire*, 15.

35. Thomas Jefferson to John Jay, Aug. 23, 1785, in *Writings*, 818; Jefferson to Archibald Stuart, Jan. 25, 1786, in *Writings*, 844.

36. Robert W. Tucker and David C. Hendrickson, *Empire of Liberty: The State-craft of Thomas Jefferson,* 6; Thomas Jefferson to George Washington, March 15, 1784, in *Writings,* 787.

37. George Washington, Farewell Address, in Reid, *American Rhetorical Discourse,* 220; John Adams, Inaugural Address, in *Inaugural Addresses of the Presidents of the United States,* 11.

38. Onuf, *Jefferson's Empire,* 113; Thomas Jefferson to John Taylor, June 6, 1798, in *Writings,* 1050; Jefferson to Gerry, Jan. 26, 1799, in *Writings,* 1056.

39. For representative statements, see Banning, *Jeffersonian Persuasion,* and the collection of essays in Appleby, *Liberalism;* Walter Lafeber, "Jefferson and American Foreign Policy," in Onuf, *Jeffersonian Legacies,* 389.

40. Thomas Jefferson to Thomas Pinckney, May 29, 1797, in *Writings,* 1045; Jefferson to Washington, March 15, 1784, in *Writings,* 787.

41. Colin Bonwick, Jefferson as Nationalist," in McDowell and Noble, *Reason and Republicanism,* 151.

42. Onuf, *Jefferson's Empire,* 107.

43. Jefferson to Granger, Aug. 13, 1800, in *Writings,* 1078.

44. Thomas Jefferson to Elbridge Gerry, May 13, 1797, in *Writings,* 1043–44.

45. Tucker and Hendrickson, *Liberty,* 18; Thomas Jefferson, quoted in Tucker and Hendrickson, *Liberty,* 15; Jefferson to George Rogers Clark, Dec. 25, 1779, quoted in Boyd, "Empire of Liberty," 189.

46. Tucker and Hendrickson, *Liberty,* 3–4.

47. French and Ayers, "The Strange Career of Thomas Jefferson," 418; James Truslow Adams, *Jeffersonian Principles and Hamiltonian Principles,* vi; Lincoln, quoted in Merrill Peterson, "Afterward," in Onuf, *Jeffersonian Legacies,* 464.

Chapter 3. *"The Circle of Our Felicities": Rhetorical Dimensions of the First Inaugural Address*

1. Brodie, *Intimate History,* 446; *Aurora,* March 6, 1801, 2, 4; Matthew Carey, Speech of Thomas Jefferson, Philadelphia, 1801, i.

2. *National Intelligencer,* March 16, 1801; *United States Oracle,* April 4, 1801, 1.

3. Robert A. Ferguson, *Law and Letters in American Culture,* 78.

4. Thomas Jefferson to Thomas Jefferson Randolph, Nov. 24, 1808, in *Writings,* 1194, 1195.

5. Thomas Jefferson, "Autobiography," in *Writings*, 4.

6. For a useful treatment of Jefferson's literary career, see especially Douglas L. Wilson, "Jefferson and the Republic of Letters," in Onuf, *Jeffersonian Legacies*, 50–76. Jefferson to Robert Skipworth, Aug. 3, 1771, in *Writings*, 742; Jefferson to Peter Carr, Sept. 7, 1814, *Writings*, 1347, 1352.

7. On Jefferson's library, see especially James Gilreath and Douglas L. Wilson, eds., *Thomas Jefferson's Library;* and E. Millicent Sowerby, comp., *Catalogue of the Library of Thomas Jefferson.*

8. Wilbur Samuel Howell, "The Declaration of Independence and Eighteenth-Century Logic," *William and Mary Quarterly* 18 (1961): 463–84; Fliegelman, *Declaring Independence;* S. Gustafson, *Eloquence is Power.*

9. North American Review 45 (1850), 445.

10. Joyce Appleby, *Inheriting the Revolution: The First Generation of Americans.*

11. Ibid., 36; Gordon Wood, *The Radicalism of the American Revolution*, 363.

12. For a succinct account of Jefferson's religious thought, see especially Paul Conkin, "The Religious Pilgrimage of Thomas Jefferson," in Onuf, *Jeffersonian Legacies*, 19–49.

13. Thomas Jefferson to Henry Lee, May 8, 1825, in *Writings*, 1501.

14. John Winthrop, "A Model of Christian Charity," in Reid, *American Rhetorical Discourse*, 34; Israel Evans, "A Sermon, Delivered at Concord," in Sandoz, *Political Sermons*, 1077; on the theme of America as a chosen people, see especially Sacvan Bercovitch, *Rites of Assent: Transformations in the Symbolic Construction of America.*

15. Samuel Danforth, "A Brief Recognition of New England's Errand into the Wilderness," in Reid, *American Rhetorical Discourse*, 51; Samuel Miller, "A Sermon, Preached in New-York," in Sandoz, *Political Sermons*, 1166.

16. Jonathan Mayhew, "The Snare Broken," *Political Sermons*, 262; David Tappan, "A Sermon Preached Before His Excellency John Hancock, Esq.," ibid., 1126.

17. David Waldstreicher, *'In the Midst of Perpetual Fetes': The Making of American Nationalism, 1776–1820*, 12.

18. James M. Farrell, review of *Celebrating the Fourth: Independence Day and the Rites of Nationalism in the Early Republic*, by Len Travers, *Rhetoric and Public Affairs* 2 (1999): 148.

19. Silverman, *Cultural History*, 605.

20. *Aurora*, March 18, 1801, 2; quoted in *Connecticut Courant*, June 22, 1801, 1.

21. Benedict Anderson, *Imagined Communities: Reflections on the Origin and Spread of Nationalism*, 44.

22. Waldstreicher, *Perpetual Fetes*, chaps. 3–4.

23. Bailyn, *Ideological Origins*, 1.

24. Ellis, *Founding Brothers*, 68.

25. Stephen E. Lucas, "Genre Criticism and Historical Context: The Case of George Washington's First Inaugural Address," *The Southern Speech Communication Journal* 51 (1986): 363, 368.

26. Quoted in Malone, *Jefferson the Virginian*, 391; Wood, "Trials and Tribulations of Thomas Jefferson," 401.

27. John Adams, *Works of John Adams*, 2:514; Carl Becker, *The Declaration of Independence: A Study in the History of Political Ideas*, 196.

28. *North American Review* 31 (1830), 34; Ellis, *American Sphinx*, 225.

29. Kennedy, *Aristotle on Rhetoric*, 38.

30. Jefferson to Mazzei, April 24, 1796, in *Writings*, 1036.

31. Jefferson to Priestly, March 21, 1801, in *Writings*, 1086.

32. Thomas Jefferson, Declaration of Independence, in *Writings*, 19; Thomas Jefferson to Edward Carrington, Jan. 16, 1787, in ibid., 880; Thomas Jefferson to James Madison, Dec. 28, 1794, in ibid., 1015; Jefferson, Draft of Kentucky Resolutions, in *Writings*, 451.

33. Thomas Jefferson to Abigail Adams, Feb. 22, 1787, in *Writings*, 890.

34. Kennedy, *Aristotle on Rhetoric*, 222.

35. Thomas Paine, "Common Sense," in Reid, *American Rhetorical Discourse*, 121; John Quincy Adams, *Lectures on Rhetoric and Oratory*, 10.

36. Cicero, *De oratore*, in Thomas W. Benson and Michael Prosser, eds., *Readings in Classical Rhetoric*, 224, 243; Blair, quoted in James L. Golden and Edward P. J. Corbett, eds., *The Rhetoric of Blair, Campbell, and Whately*, 67.

37. Jefferson to Dickinson, March 6, 1801, in *Writings*, 1084.

38. Adams, *The Works of John Adams*, 1:616; Becker, *Declaration*, 218–19.

Epilogue

1. *National Intelligencer*, March 9, 1801, 3.

2. Peterson, *Jefferson Image*, 457.

Bibliography

Collections

Adams, Charles Francis, ed. *The Memoirs of John Quincy Adams.* 12 vols. Boston, 1874.

———, ed. *The Works of John Adams.* 2 vols. Boston: Little, Brown, and Co., 1856.

Burke, Edmund. *The Works of Edmund Burke.* 12 vols. Boston: Little, Brown. 1889.

Cottret, Bernard, ed. *Bolingbroke's Political Writings.* New York: St. Martin's, 1977.

Ford, Worthington C., ed. *Writings of John Quincy Adams.* 7 vols. New York: Macmillan Co., 1914.

Hendel, Charles W., ed. *David Hume's Political Essays.* New York: Bobbs-Merrill Co. Inc., 1953.

Inaugural Addresses of the Presidents of the United States. Washington, D.C.: U.S. Government Printing Office, 1961.

King, Charles R., ed. *The Life and Correspondence of Rufus King.* New York: G. P. Putman's Sons, 1896.

Malone, Dumas, ed. *Correspondence Between Thomas Jefferson and Pierre Samuel Du Pont Nemour, 1798–1817.* Translated by Linwood Lehman. New York and Boston: Mifflin Co., 1930.

Peterson, Merrill D., ed. *Thomas Jefferson: Writings.* New York: Library of America, 1984.

Reid, Ronald F., ed. *American Rhetorical Discourse.* Prospect Heights: Waveland, Press, 1995.

Sandoz, Ellis, ed. *Political Sermons of the Founding Era, 1730–1815.* Indianapolis: Liberty Press, 1991.

Sutherland, Lucy, ed. *The Correspondence of Edmund Burke*. Chicago: University of Chicago Press, 1969.

Syrett, Harold C., ed. *The Papers of Alexander Hamilton*. 27 vols. New York: Columbia University Press, 1961–1981.

Pamphlets

Carey, Matthew. Speech of Thomas Jefferson. Philadelphia, 1801.

Coxe, Tench. *A View of the United States of America*. Philadelphia, 1795.

Dwight, Theodore. *The Character of Thomas Jefferson*. Boston: Week, Jordan, and Co., 1830.

Gordon, Thomas, and John Trenchard. *Cato's Letters*. London, 1733.

Taylor, John. *Definition of Parties; or the Political Effects of the Paper System Considered*. Philadelphia, 1794.

Sources

Adams, Henry. *History of the United States of America*. 2 vols. New York: Charles Scribner's Sons, 1889.

Adams, James Truslow. *Jeffersonian Principles and Hamiltonian Principles*. Boston: Little, Brown, and Co., 1932.

Adams, John. "Autobiography." In *The Works of John Adams*, edited by Charles Francis Adams. Boston: Little, Brown, and Co., 1856.

Adams, John Quincy. *Lectures on Rhetoric and Oratory*. Delmar: Scholars' Facsimiles and Reprints, 1997.

Anderson, Benedict. *Imagined Communities: Reflections on the Origin and Spread of Nationalism*. Rev. ed. London and New York: Verso, 1991.

Appleby, Joyce. *Capitalism and a New Social Order: The Republican Vision of the 1790s*. New York: New York University Press, 1984.

———. *Inheriting the Revolution: The First Generation of Americans*. Cambridge: Harvard University Press, 2000.

———. "Jefferson and His Complex Legacy." In *Jeffersonian Legacies*, edited by Peter Onuf, 1–16. Charlottesville: University Press of Virginia, 1993.

———. *Liberalism and Republicanism in the Historical Imagination*. Cambridge: Harvard University Press, 1992.

Bailyn, Bernard. *The Ideological Origins of the American Revolution.* Cambridge: Harvard University Press, 1974.

Banning, Lance. *The Jeffersonian Persuasion: Evolution of a Party Ideology.* Ithaca: Cornell University Press, 1978.

Becker, Carl. *The Declaration of Independence: A Study in the History of Political Ideas.* New York: Vintage Books, 1942.

Benson, Thomas W., ed. *American Rhetoric: Contexts and Criticism.* Carbondale: Southern Illinois University Press, 1989.

Benson, Thomas W., and Michael Prosser, eds. *Readings in Classical Rhetoric.* Davis: Hermagoras Press, 1987.

Bercovitch, Sacvan. *Rites of Assent: Transformations in the Symbolic Construction of America.* New York: Routledge, 1993.

Blair, Hugh. "Lectures on Rhetoric and Belles Lettres." In *The Rhetoric of Blair, Campbell, and Whately,* edited by James Golden, and Edward P. J. Corbett, 30–137. New York: Holt, Rinehart, and Winston, 1968.

Bolingbroke, Henry St. John Viscount. "A Dissertation on Parties." In *Bolingbroke's Political Writings,* edited by Bernard Cottret. New York: St. Martin's, 1977.

Bonwick, Colin. "Jefferson as Nationalist. In *Reason and Republicanism: Thomas Jefferson's Legacy of Liberty,* edited by Gary L. McDowell, and Sharon L. Noble, 149–68. New York: Rowan and Littlefield Publishers, Inc., 1997.

Boorstin, Daniel J. *The Lost World of Thomas Jefferson.* Boston: Beacon Press, 1960.

Bowers, Claude G. *Jefferson in Power: The Death Struggle of the Federalists.* Boston: Houghton Mifflin, 1964.

Boyd, Julian P. "Thomas Jefferson's 'Empire of Liberty.'" In *Thomas Jefferson: A Profile,* edited by Merrill D. Peterson, 178–94. New York: Hill and Wang, 1967.

Brodie, Fawn M. *Thomas Jefferson: An Intimate History.* New York: W. W. Norton, 1974.

Buel, Richard, Jr. *Securing the Revolution: Ideology in American Politics, 1789–1815.* Ithaca: Cornell University Press, 1972.

Burke, Edmund. *Thoughts on the Cause of the Present Discontents.* In *The Works of Edmund Burke,* 433–537. 12 vols. Boston: Little, Brown. 1889.

Chambers, William Nisbet. *Political Parties in the New Nation: The American Experience, 1776–1809.* New York: Oxford University Press, 1963.

Cmiel, Kenneth. *Democratic Eloquence: The Fight Over Popular Speech in Nineteenth-Century America.* Berkeley: University of California Press, 1989.

Cohen, William. "Thomas Jefferson and the Problem of Slavery." *Journal of American History* 56 (1969): 503–26.

Colbourn, H. Trevor. *The Lamp of Experience: Whig History and the Intellectual Origins of the American Revolution.* Chapel Hill: University of North Carolina Press, 1965.

Conkin, Paul. "The Religious Pilgrimage of Thomas Jefferson." In *Jeffersonian Legacies,* edited by Peter Onuf, 19–49. Charlottesville: University Press of Virginia, 1993.

Conrad, Stephen A. "Putting Rights Talk in its Place: The Summary View Revisited." In *Jeffersonian Legacies,* edited by Peter Onuf, 254–80. Charlottesville: University Press of Virginia, 1993.

Cunningham, Noble E., Jr. *The Jeffersonian Republicans: The Formation of Party Organization, 1789–1801.* Chapel Hill: University of North Carolina Press, 1957.

———. *The Jeffersonian Republicans in Power: Party Operations, 1801–1809.* Chapel Hill: University of North Carolina Press, 1963.

Danforth, Samuel. "A Brief Recognition of New England's Errand into the Wilderness." In *American Rhetorical Discourse,* edited by Ronald F. Reid, 38–52. Prospect Heights: Waveland, Press, 1995.

Davis, Richard Beale. *Intellectual Life in the Colonial South, 1685–1763.* Knoxville: University of Tennessee Press, 1978.

Dewey, John. *The Living Thoughts of Thomas Jefferson.* Philadelphia: David McKay Co., 1940.

Elkins, Stanley, and Eric McKitrick. *The Age of Federalism.* New York: Oxford University Press, 1993.

Ellis, Joseph. *American Sphinx: The Character of Thomas Jefferson.* New York: Vintage, 1998.

———. *Founding Brothers: The Revolutionary Generation.* New York: Alfred A. Knopf, 2000.

Engeman, Thomas S., ed. *Thomas Jefferson and the Politics of Nature.* Notre Dame: Notre Dame University Press, 2000.

Evans, Israel. "A Sermon Delivered at Concord." In *Political Sermons of the Founding Era, 1730–1815,* edited by Ellis Sandoz, 1061–78. Indianapolis: Liberty Press, 1991.

Farrell, James M. Review of *Celebrating the Fourth: Independence Day and the Rites of Nationalism in the Early Republic,* by Len Travers. *Rhetoric and Public Affairs* 2 (1999): 147–49.

Ferguson, Robert A. *Law and Letters in American Culture.* Cambridge: Harvard University Press, 1984.

———. "'We Hold These Truths': Strategies of Control in the Literature of the Founders." In *Reconstructing American Literary History,* edited by Sacvan Bercovitch, 1–29. Cambridge: Harvard University Press, 1986.

Fliegelman, Jay. *Declaring Independence: Jefferson, Natural Language, and the Culture of Performance.* Stanford: Stanford University Press, 1993.

Fowler, Robert Booth. "Mythologies of a Founder." In *Thomas Jefferson and the Politics of Nature,* edited by Thomas S. Engeman, 123–41. Notre Dame: Notre Dame University Press, 2000.

French, Scot A., and Edward L. Ayers, "The Strange Career of Thomas Jefferson: Race and Slavery in American Memory, 1943–1993." In *Jeffersonian Legacies,* edited by Peter Onuf. Charlottesville: University Press of Virginia, 1993.

Gilreath, James, and Douglas Wilson, eds. *Thomas Jefferson's Library.* Washington: Library of Congress, 1989.

Golden, James, and Edward P. J. Corbett, eds. *The Rhetoric of Blair, Campbell, and Whately.* New York: Holt, Rinehart, and Winston, 1968.

Gordon-Reed, Annette. *Thomas Jefferson and Sally Hemings: An American Controversy.* Charlottesville: University Press of Virginia, 1997.

Gustafson, Sandra M. *Eloquence is Power: Oratory and Performance in Early America.* Chapel Hill: University of North Carolina Press, 2000.

Gustafson, Thomas. *Representative Words: Politics, Literature, and the American Language, 1776–1865.* Cambridge: Cambridge University Press, 1992.

Hitchcock, Enos. "An Oration in Commemoration of the Independence of the United States of America." In *Political Sermons of the Founding Era, 1730–1815,* edited by Ellis Sandoz, 1169–83. Indianapolis: Liberty Press, 1991.

Hofstadter, Richard. *The Idea of a Party System: The Rise of Legitimate Opposition in the United States, 1780–1840.* Berkeley: University of California Press, 1969.

Howe, John R., Jr. "Republican Thought and the Political Violence of the 1790s." *American Quarterly* 19 (1967): 147–65.

Howell, Wilbur Samuel. "The Declaration of Independence and Eighteenth-Century Logic. *William and Mary Quarterly* 18 (1961): 463–84.

————. *Eighteenth-Century British Logic and Rhetoric.* Princeton: Princeton University Press, 1971.

Hume, David. "Of Parties in General." In *David Hume's Political Essays,* edited by Charles W. Hendel. New York: Bobbs-Merrill Co. Inc., 1953.

Kennedy, George A. *Aristotle on Rhetoric: A Theory of Civic Discourse.* New York: Oxford University Press, 1991.

Koch, Adrienne, and Harry Ammon. "The Virginia and Kentucky Resolutions: An Episode in Jefferson's and Madison's Defense of Civil Liberties." *William and Mary Quarterly* 5 (1948): 145–76.

Kramer, Michael. *Imagining Language in America: From the Revolution to the Civil War.* Princeton: Princeton University Press, 1992.

Lafeber, Walter. "Jefferson and American Foreign Policy." In *Jeffersonian Legacies,* edited by Peter Onuf, 370–91. Charlottesville: University Press of Virginia, 1993.

Lewis, Jan Ellen, and Peter S. Onuf, eds. *Sally Hemings and Thomas Jefferson: History, Memory, and Civic Culture.* Charlottesville: University Press of Virginia, 1999.

Looby, Christopher. *Voicing America: Language, Literary Form, and the Origins of the United States.* Chicago: University of Chicago Press, 1996.

Lucas, Stephen. "Genre Criticism and Historical Context: The Case of George Washington's First Inaugural Address." *The Southern Speech Communication Journal* 51 (1986): 354–70.

————. "Justifying America: The Declaration of Independence as a Rhetorical Document." In *American Rhetoric: Contexts and Criticism,* edited by Thomas W. Benson, 67–130. Carbondale: Southern Illinois University Press, 1989.

Maier, Pauline. *American Scripture: Making the Declaration of Independence.* New York: Vintage, 1998.

Malone, Dumas. *Jefferson and the Ordeal of Liberty.* Boston: Little, Brown, and Co., 1962.

————. *Jefferson the President: First Term, 1801–1805.* Boston: Little, Brown, and Co., 1970.

————. *Jefferson and the Rights of Man.* Boston: Little, Brown, and Co., 1950.

————. *Jefferson the Virginian.* Boston: Little, Brown, and Co., 1948.

Mathews, Richard K. *The Radical Politics of Thomas Jefferson: A Revisionist View.* Lawrence: University of Kansas Press, 1984.

Mayer, David N. *The Constitutional Thought of Thomas Jefferson.* Charlottesville: University Press of Virginia, 1994.

Mayhew, Jonathan. "The Snare Broken." In *Political Sermons of the Founding Era, 1730–1815,* edited by Ellis Sandoz, 235–64. Indianapolis: Liberty Press, 1991.

McCoy, Drew R. *The Elusive Republic: Political Economy in Jeffersonian America.* Chapel Hill: University of North Carolina Press, 1980.

McDowell, Gary L., and Sharon L. Noble, eds. *Reason and Republicanism: Thomas Jefferson's Legacy of Liberty.* New York: Rowan and Littlefield Publishers, Inc., 1997.

Miller, Charles A. *Jefferson and Nature: An Interpretation.* Baltimore: The Johns Hopkins University Press, 1988.

Miller, Samuel. "A Sermon Preached in New-York." In *Political Sermons of the Founding Era, 1730–1815,* edited by Ellis Sandoz, 1153–67. Indianapolis: Liberty Press, 1991.

Onuf, Peter. *Jefferson's Empire: The Language of American Nationhood.* Charlottesville: University Press of Virginia, 2000.

———. "The Scholars' Jefferson." *William and Mary Quarterly* 50 (1993): 671–99.

———, ed. *Jeffersonian Legacies.* Charlottesville: University Press of Virginia, 1993.

Paine, Thomas. "Common Sense." In *American Rhetorical Discourse,* edited by Ronald F. Reid, 120–32. Prospect Heights: Waveland, Press, 1995.

Peterson, Merrill D. "Afterward." In *Jeffersonian Legacies,* edited by Peter Onuf, 457–64. Charlottesville: University Press of Virginia, 1993.

———. *The Jefferson Image in the American Mind.* New York: Oxford University Press, 1960.

———. *Thomas Jefferson and the New Nation: A Biography.* New York: Oxford University Press, 1970.

———, ed. *Thomas Jefferson: A Profile.* New York: Hill and Wang, 1967.

Pole, J. R. "Jefferson and the Pursuit of Equality." In *Reason and Republicanism: Thomas Jefferson's Legacy of Liberty,* edited by Gary L. McDowell, and Sharon L. Noble, 219–30. New York: Rowan and Littlefield Publishers, Inc., 1997.

Randall, Henry. *The Life of Thomas Jefferson.* New York: Derby and Jackson, 1858.

Read, James H. *Power Versus Liberty: Madison, Hamilton, Wilson, and Jefferson.* Charlottesville: University Press of Virginia, 2000.

Reid, Ronald F. *American Rhetorical Discourse.* Prospects Heights: Waveland Press, 1995.

Robbins, Caroline. *The Eighteenth-Century Commonwealthman.* Cambridge: Harvard University Press, 1959.

Sandoz, Ellis. *Political Sermons of the Founding Era, 1730–1805.* Indianapolis: Liberty Press, 1991.

Sharp, James Roger. *American Politics in the Early Republic: The New Nation in Crisis.* New Haven: Yale University Press, 1993.

Sheldon, Garrett Ward. *The Political Philosophy of Thomas Jefferson.* Baltimore: Johns Hopkins University Press, 1991.

Silverman, Kenneth. *A Cultural History of the American Revolution.* New York: Crowell, 1976.

Stout, Harry S. *The New England Soul: Preaching and Religious Culture in Colonial New England.* New York: Oxford University Press, 1986.

Tappan, David. "A Sermon Preached Before His Excellency John Hancock, Esq." In *Political Sermons of the Founding Era, 1730–1815,* edited by Ellis Sandoz, 1105–27. Indianapolis: Liberty Press, 1991.

Sowerby, E. Millicent, comp. *Catalogue of the Library of Thomas Jefferson.* Charlottesville: University Press of Virginia, 1983.

Thacher, Peter. "A Sermon Preached Before the Artillery Company." In *Political Sermons of the Founding Era, 1730–1815,* edited by Ellis Sandoz, 1129–47. Indianapolis: Liberty Press, 1991.

Travers, Len. *Celebrating the Fourth: Independence Day and the Rites of Nationalism in the Early Republic.* Amherst: University of Massachusetts Press, 1997.

Tucker, George. *The Life of Thomas Jefferson.* 2 vols. Philadelphia: Cary, Lea, and Blanchard, 1837.

Tucker, Robert W., and David C. Hendrickson. *Empire of Liberty: The Statecraft of Thomas Jefferson.* New York: Oxford University Press, 1990.

Waldstreicher, David. *'In the Midst of Perpetual Fetes': The Making of American Nationalism, 1776–1820.* Chapel Hill: University of North Carolina Press, 1997.

Warner, Michael. *The Letters of the Republic: Publication and the Public Sphere in Eighteenth-Century America.* Cambridge: Harvard University Press, 1990.

Washington, George. "Farewell Address." In *American Rhetorical Discourse,* edited by Ronald F. Reid, 209–23. Prospect Heights: Waveland, Press, 1995.

Watson, Tom. *The Life and Times of Thomas Jefferson.* New York: D. Appleton and Co., 1903.

White, Leonard D. *The Jeffersonians: A Study in Administrative History, 1801–1829.* New York: The Macmillan Company, 1951.

White, Morton. *The Philosophy of the American Revolution.* New York: Oxford University Press, 1978.

Wilson, Douglas. "Jefferson and the Republic of Letters." In *Jeffersonian Legacies,* edited by Peter Onuf, 150–76. Charlottesville: University Press of Virginia, 1993.

Wills, Gary. *Inventing America: Jefferson's Declaration of Independence.* New York: Vintage Books, 1979.

Winthrop, John. "A Model of Christian Charity." In *American Rhetorical Discourse,* edited by Ronald F. Reid, 25–35. Prospect Heights: Waveland, Press, 1995.

Wood, Gordon. *The Creation of the American Republic, 1776–1787.* Chapel Hill: University of North Carolina Press, 1969.

———. *The Radicalism of the American Revolution.* New York: Alfred A. Knopf, 1992.

———. "The Trials and Tribulations of Thomas Jefferson." In *Jeffersonian Legacies,* edited by Peter Onuf, 395–417. Charlottesville: University Press of Virginia, 1993.

Yarbrough, Jean M. *American Virtues: Thomas Jefferson on the Character of a Free People.* Lawrence: University of Kansas Press, 1998.

———. "The Moral Sense, Character Formation, and Virtue." In *Reason and Republicanism: Thomas Jefferson's Legacy of Liberty,* edited by Gary L. McDowell, and Sharon L. Noble, 271–303. New York: Rowan and Littlefield Publishers, Inc., 1997.

Zukert, Michael P. "Founder of the Natural Rights Republic." In *Thomas Jefferson and the Politics of Nature,* edited by Thomas S. Engeman, 11–58. Notre Dame: Notre Dame University Press, 2000.

———. "Response." In *Thomas Jefferson and the Politics of Nature,* edited by Thomas S. Engeman, 191–210. Notre Dame: Notre Dame University Press, 2000.

Index

Adams, Abigail, 121
Adams, Charles Francis, 9, 129
Adams, Henry, 3
Adams, James Truslow, 87
Adams, John, 9–10, 52, 112, 116
Adams, John Quincy, 12, 124
Adams, Samuel, 9
African Americans, 6, 76
Alien and Sedition Acts, 40, 46, 121
Anderson, Benedict, 106
Appleby, Joyce, 17, 29, 53, 59, 67–68,
    80, 97
Arendt, Hannah, 50
Aristotle, 7, 62, 114–15, 130
Aurora (Philadelphia), 88, 106

Bailyn, Bernard, 69–70, 108
Banning, Lance, 27, 48, 58, 66, 79
Becker, Carl, 112–13, 129–30
Beckley, John, 52
Berkeley, George, 76
Blair, Hugh, 125
Bolingbroke, Viscount, 20, 22, 23, 26
Bonwick, Colin, 55, 81
Boorstin, Daniel, 55
Boyd, Julian, 76
Brodie, Fawn, 4, 88

Burke, Edmund, 9, 19–20, 55
Burr, Aaron, 3, 32–33

Carr, Peter, 56
Charleston *Gazette,* 106
Chastellux, Marquis de, 111–12, 114
Church, Benjamin, 65
Cicero, 125
Coxe, Tenche, 75

Danforth, Samuel, 101
Declaration of Independence, 30, 51,
    62, 99, 120
Dickinson, John, 31, 36, 125
DuPont Nemour, Pierre Samuel 4, 31
Dwight, Theodore, 16

Elkins, Stanley, 18–19
Ellis, Joseph, 18, 44, 50, 54, 60, 109, 113,
    126
Evans, Israel, 100

Farrell, James, 104
Ferguson, Robert, 90
Fliegelman, Jay, 7, 94
Fowler, Robert Booth, 54
Franklin, Benjamin, 10, 58

ISBN 1-58544-252-6

90000